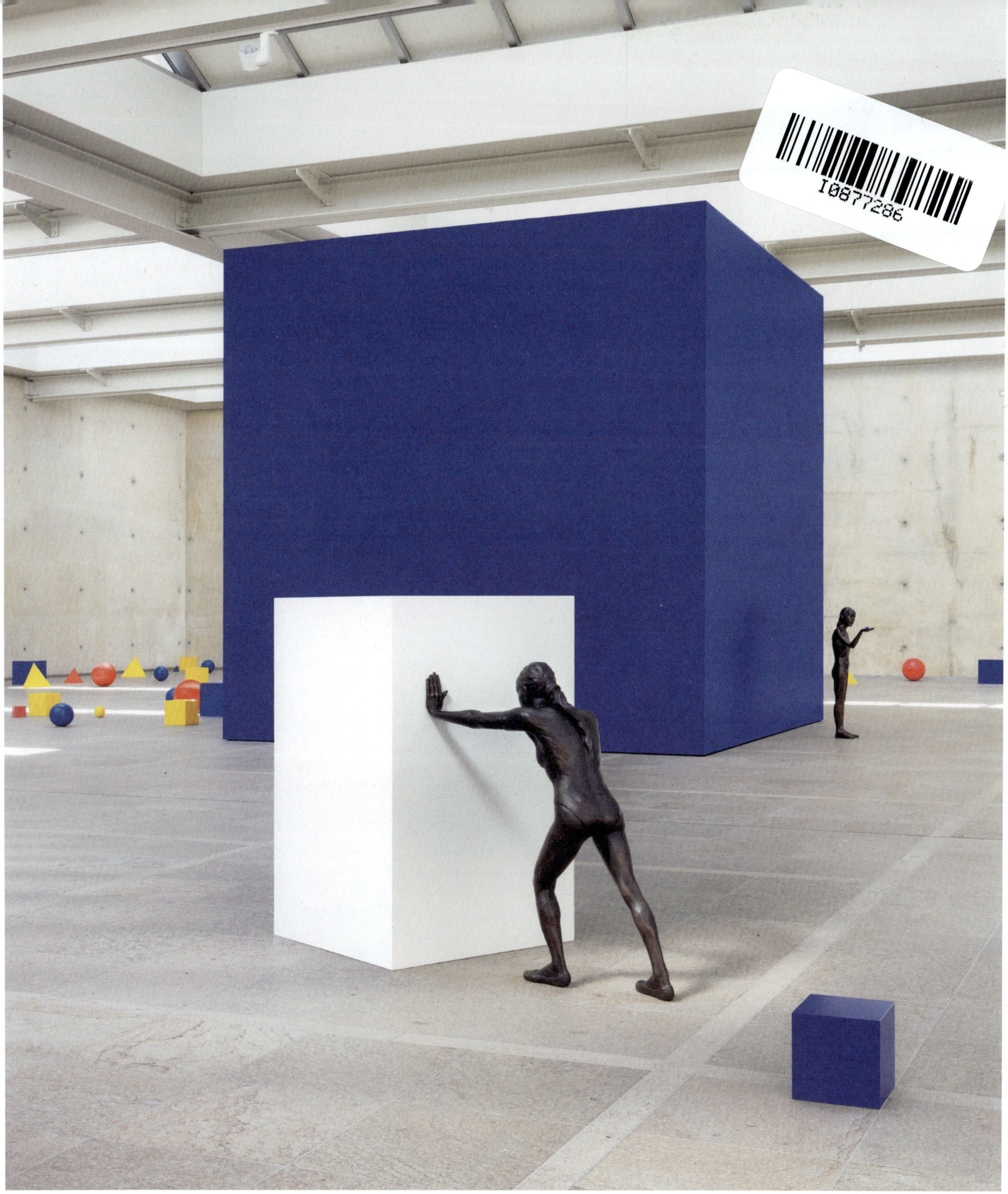

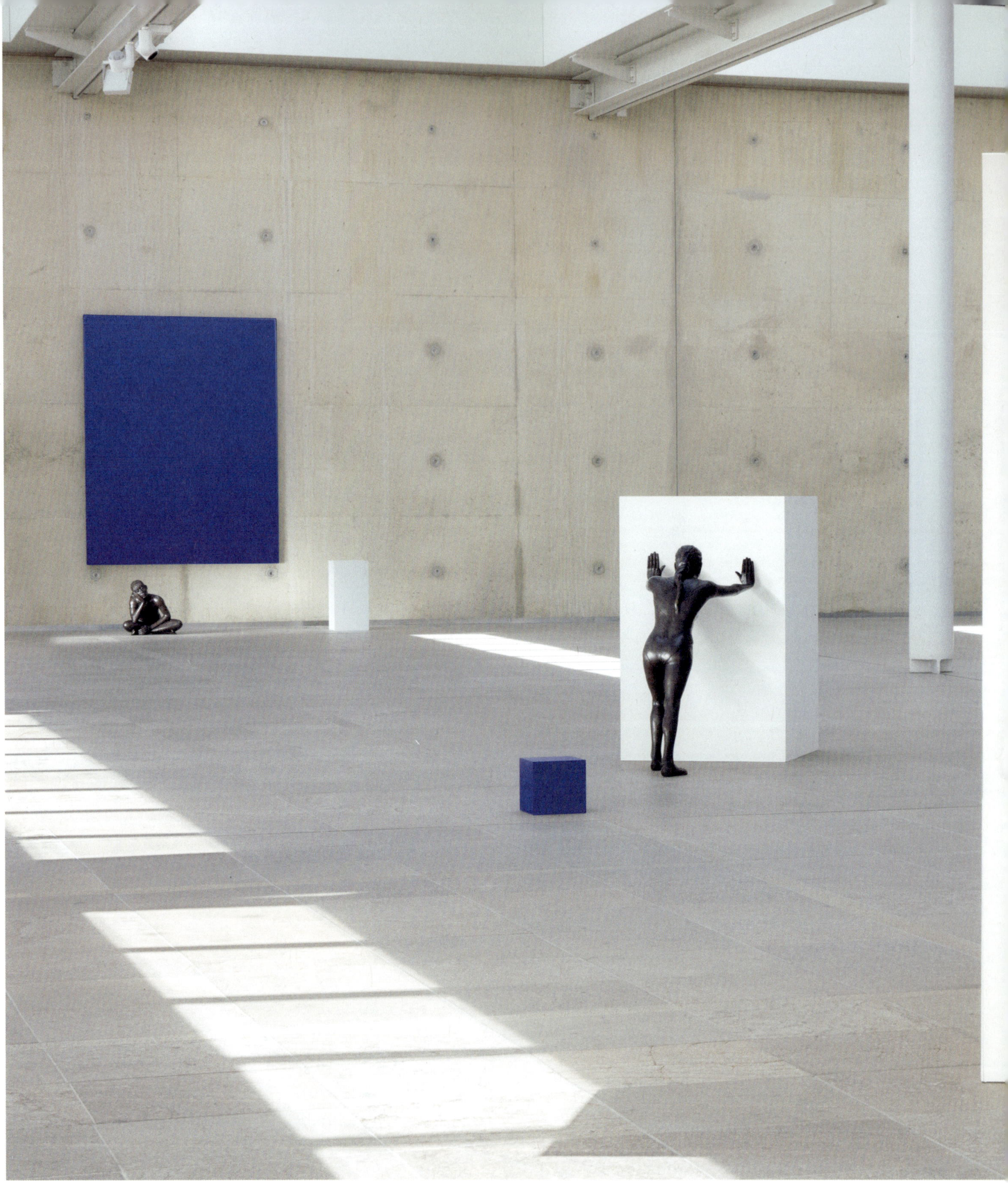

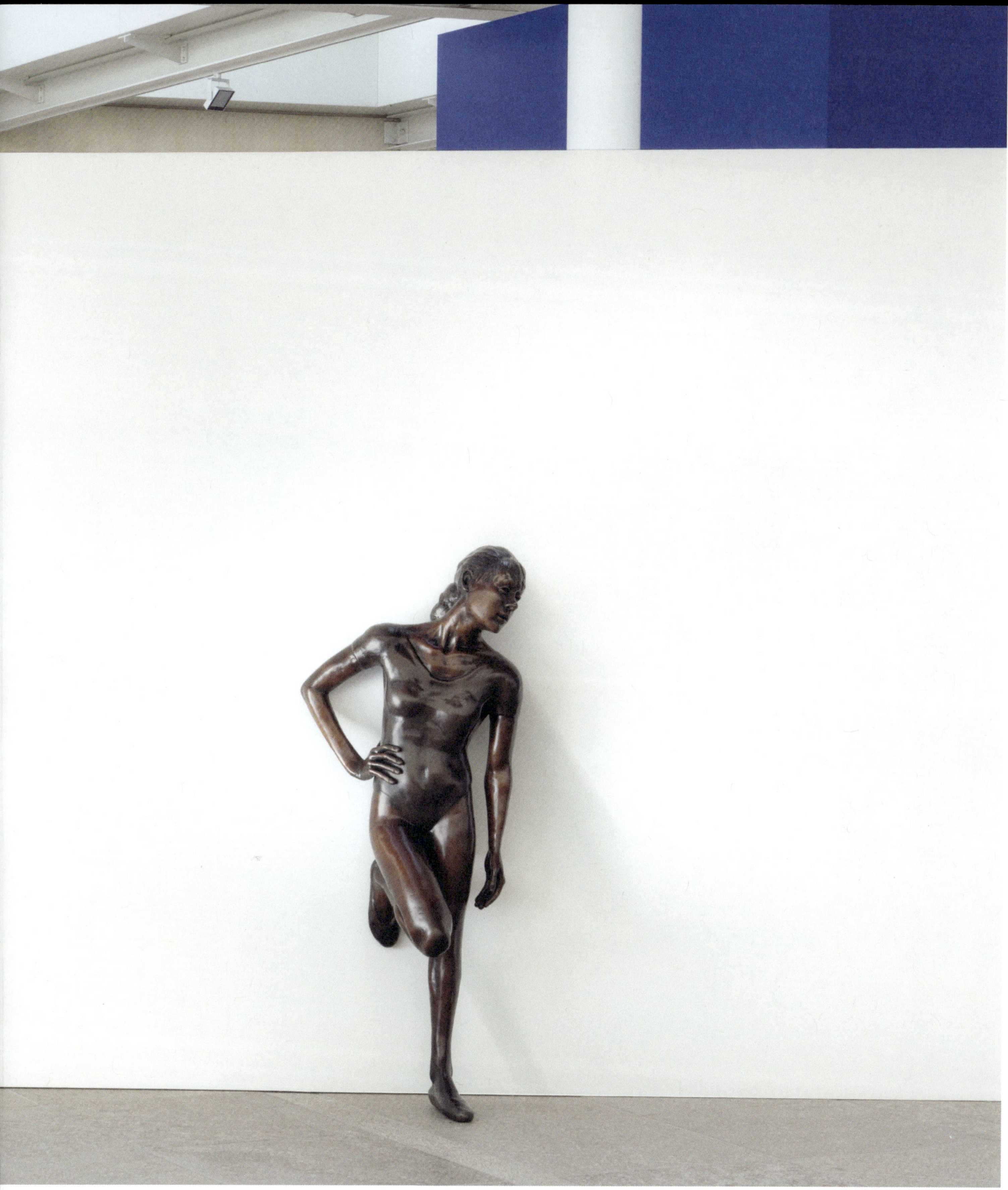

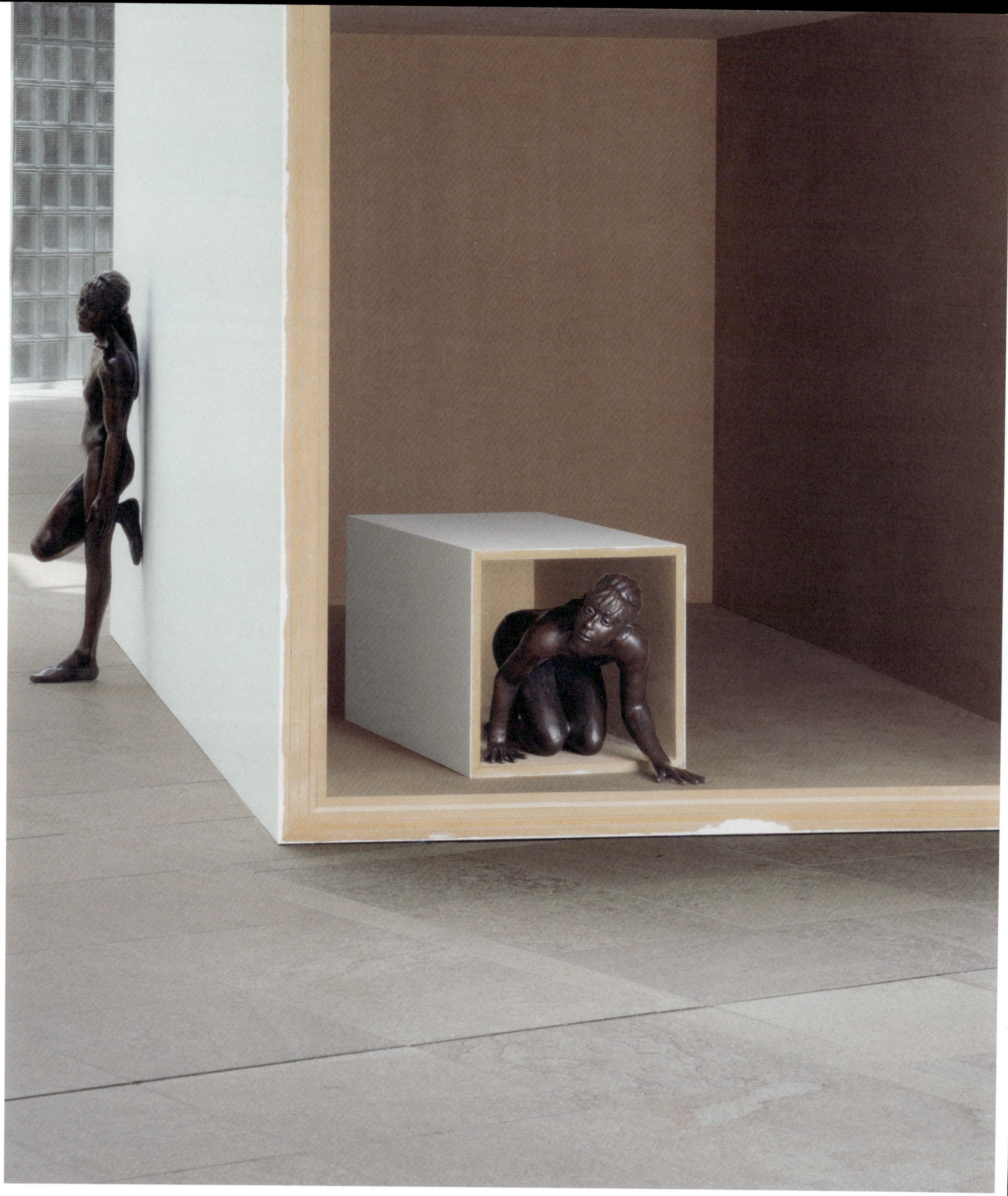

"I THINK RYAN GANDER'S WORKS ARE BEAUTIFUL. THE ARTIST'S STATUES SHOW THAT THE BALLERINAS (OR PERHAPS HE HIMSELF) SHOULD AND CAN FEEL FREE."
AMÉLIE, 14 YEARS OLD

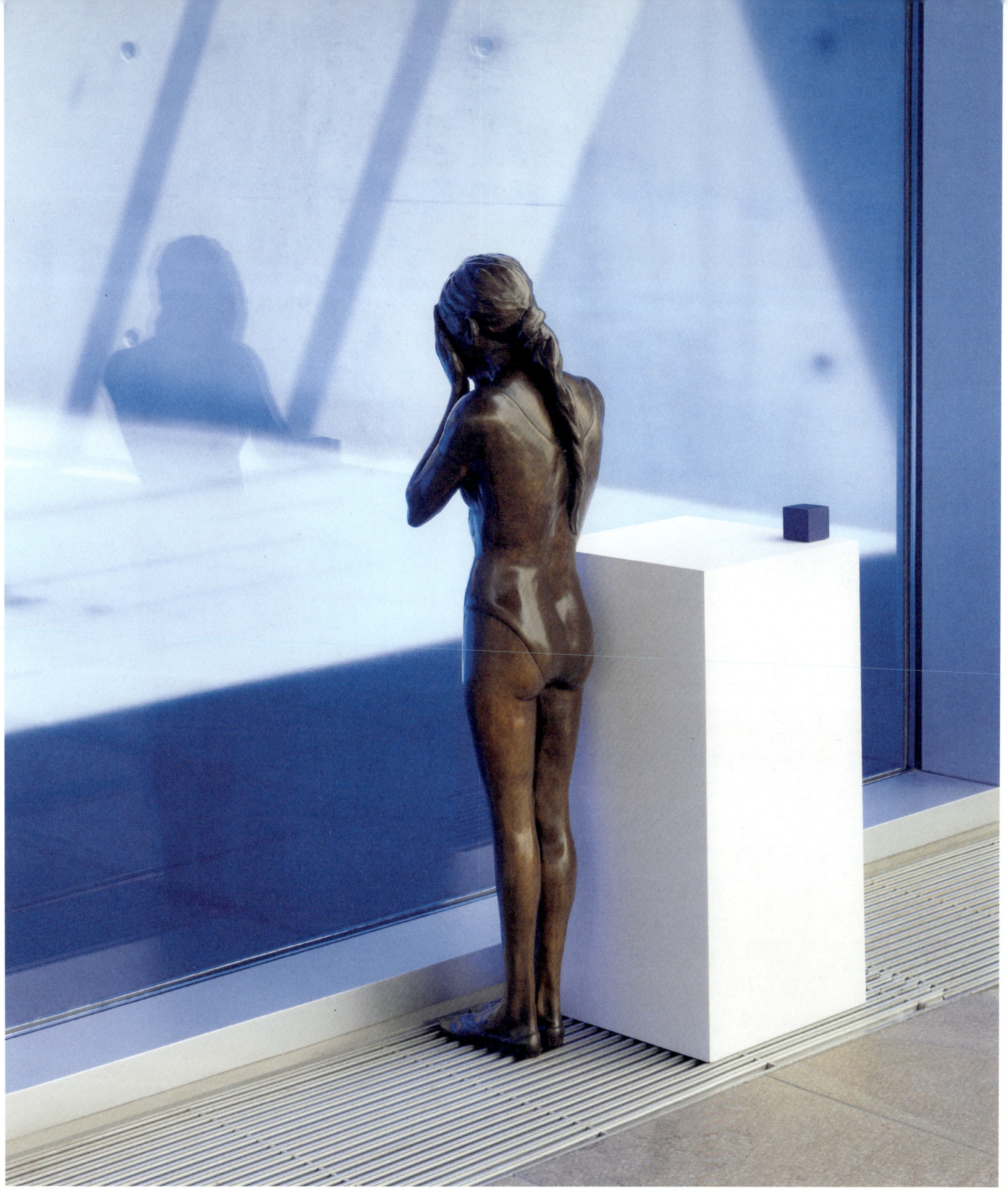

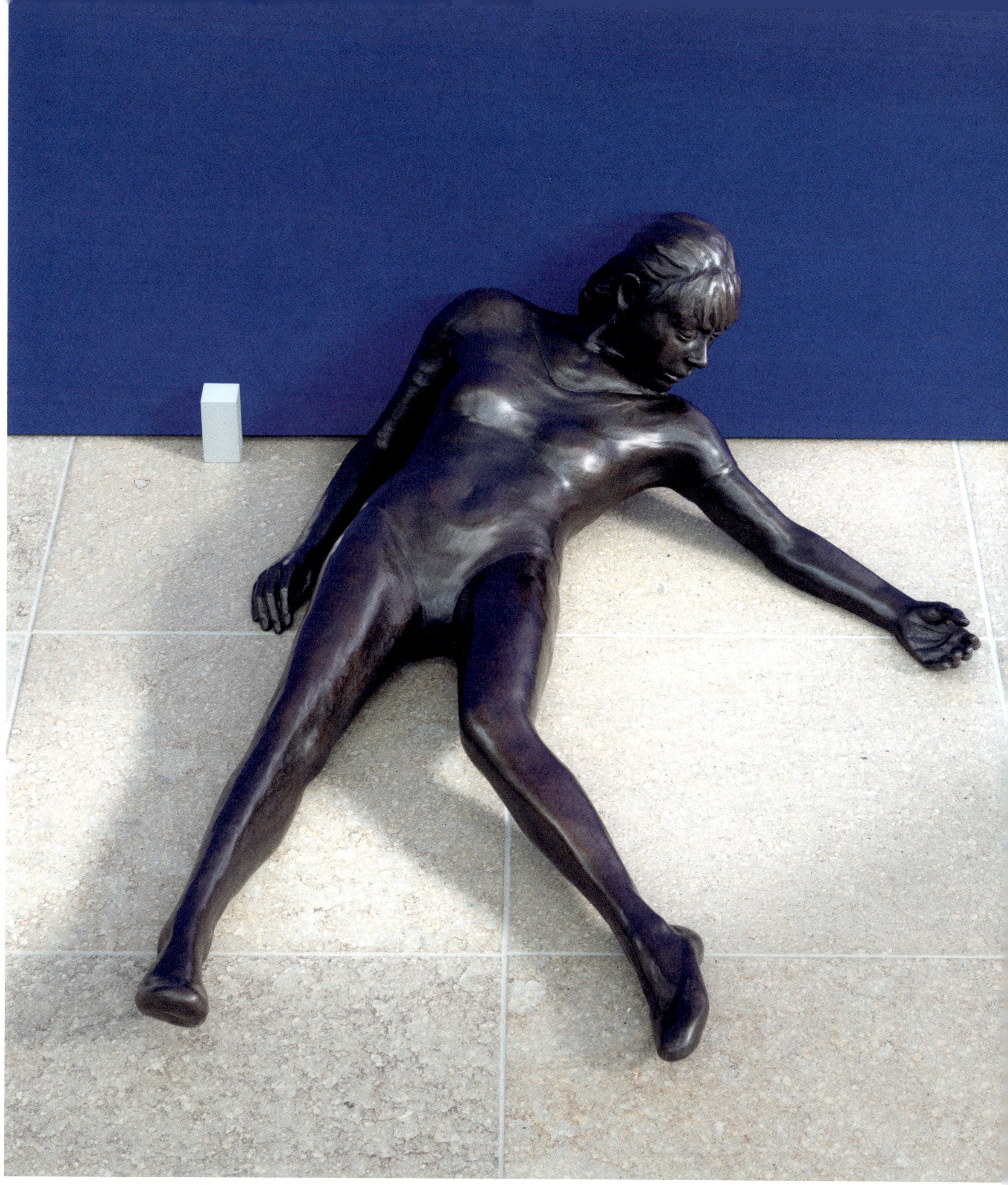

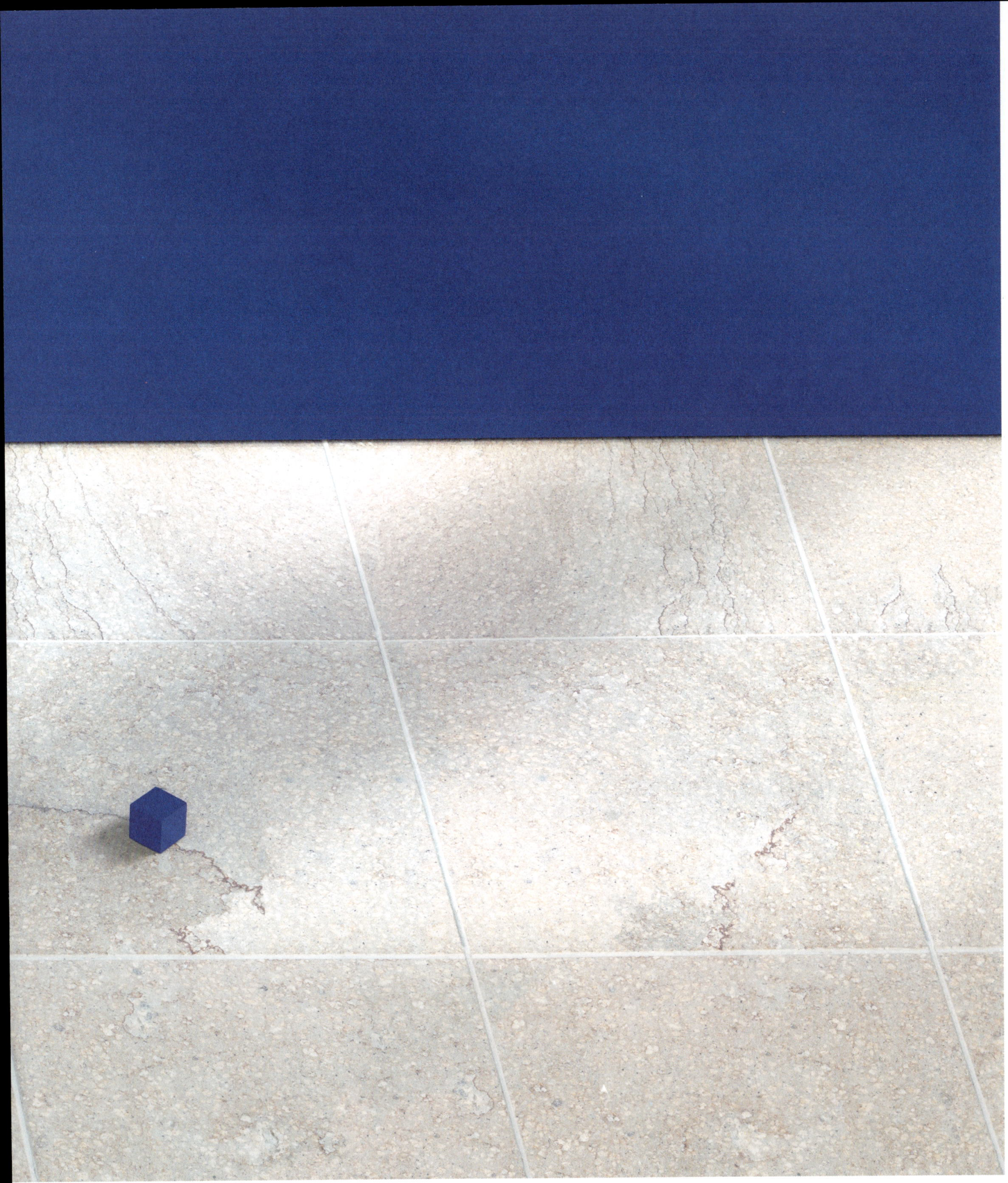

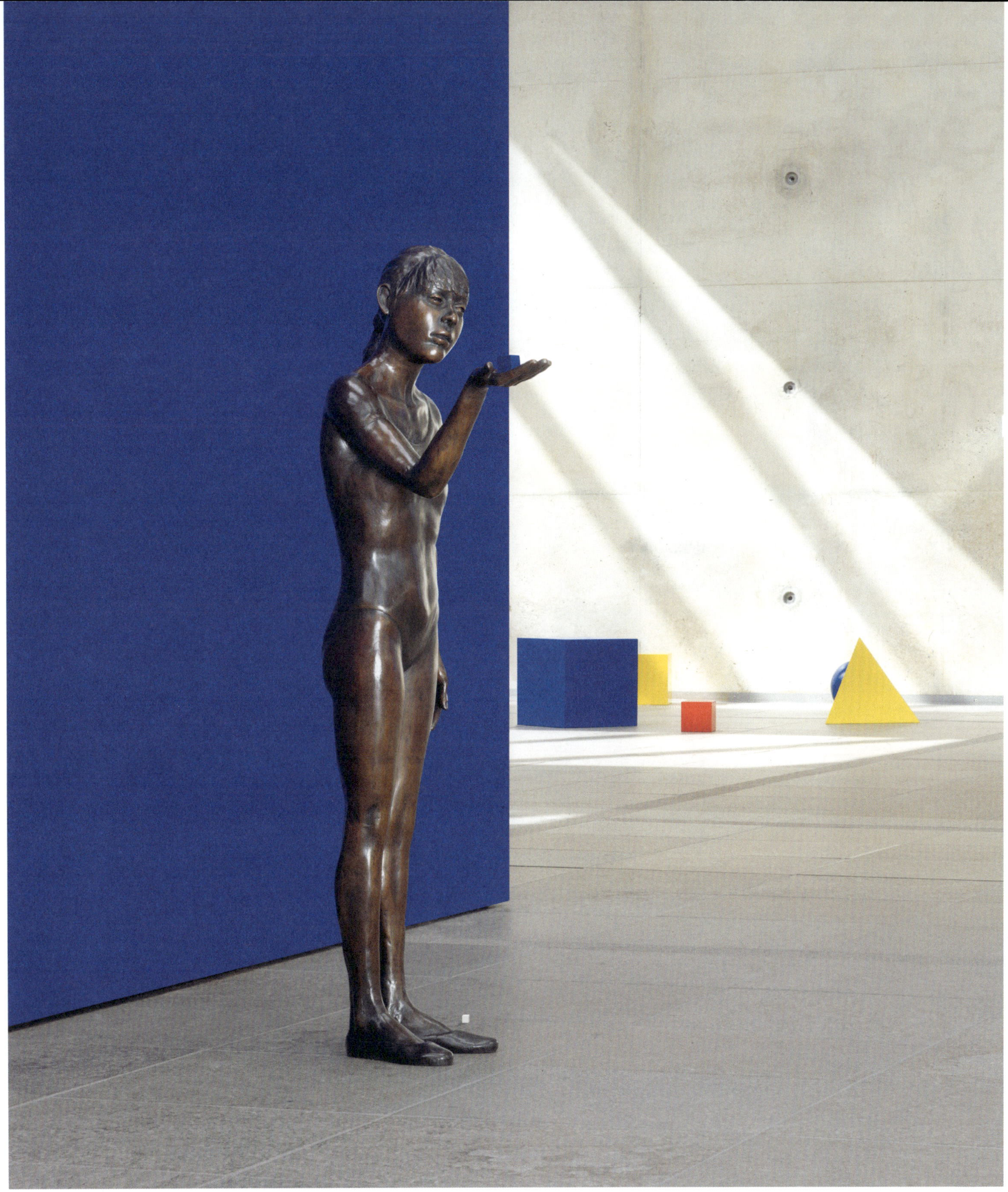

"IT SEEMS AS IF THE BALLERINA GETS HER STRENGTH FROM THE WHITE PEDESTAL AND THE BALLERINA WOULD LIKE TO OWN THE BLUE CUBE, AS IF IT'S HER OBJECTIVE."
VALENTIJN, 14 YEARS OLD

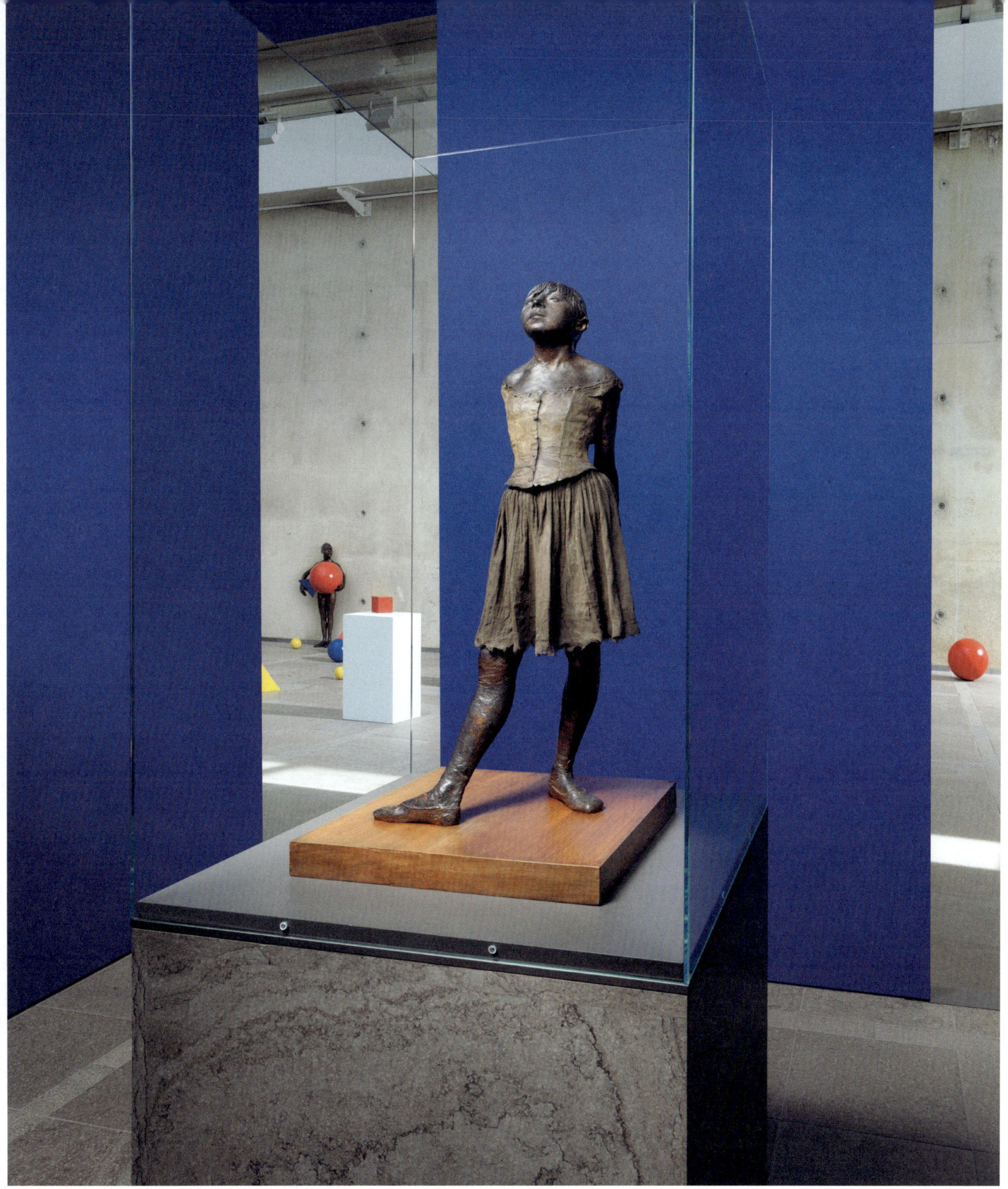

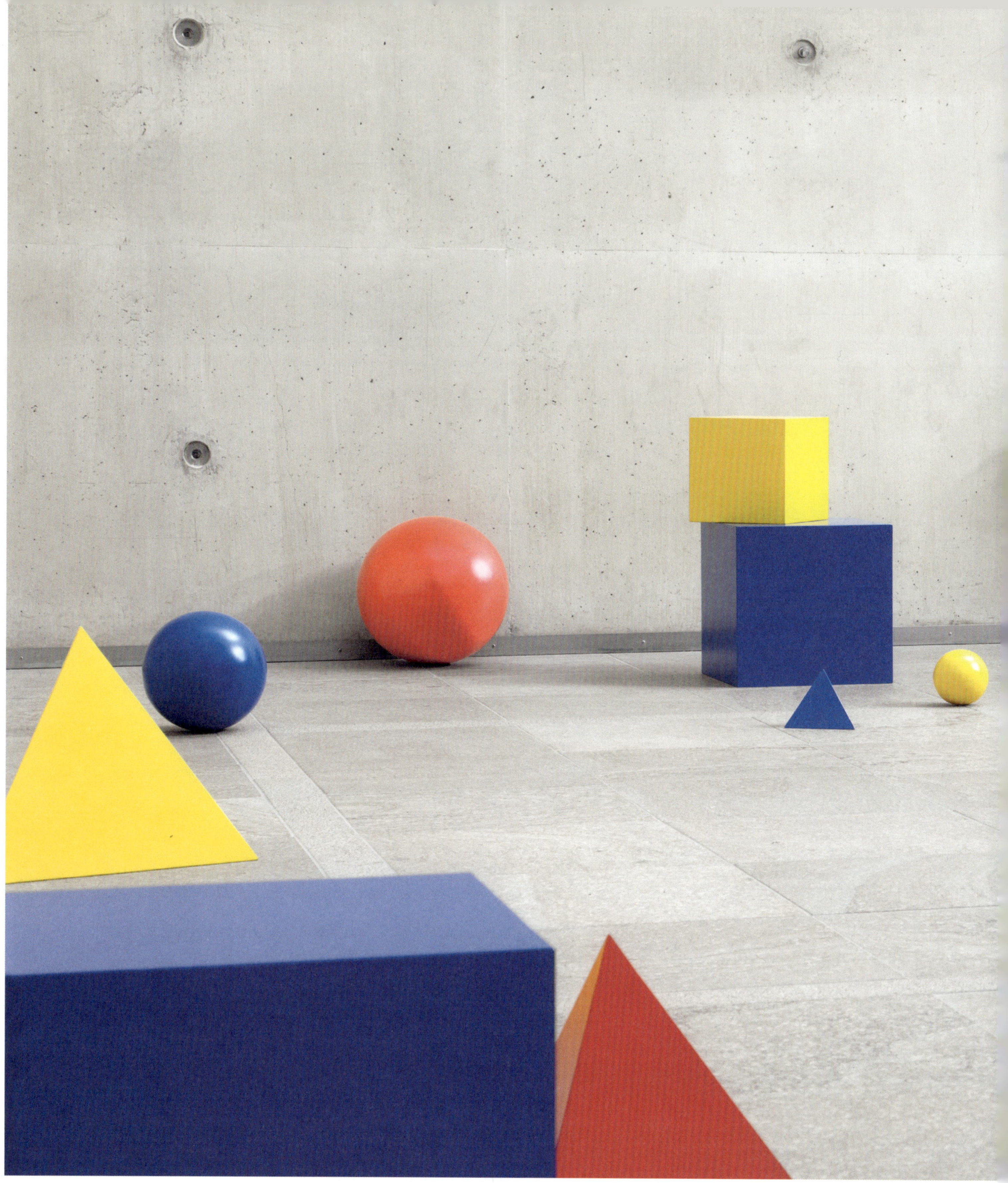

"I GET IT THAT RYAN GANDER WAS INTRIGUED BY EDGAR DEGAS'S STATUE, IT'S REALLY INSPIRING TO THINK ABOUT WHAT SHE'S FEELING."
ELISA, 14 YEARS OLD

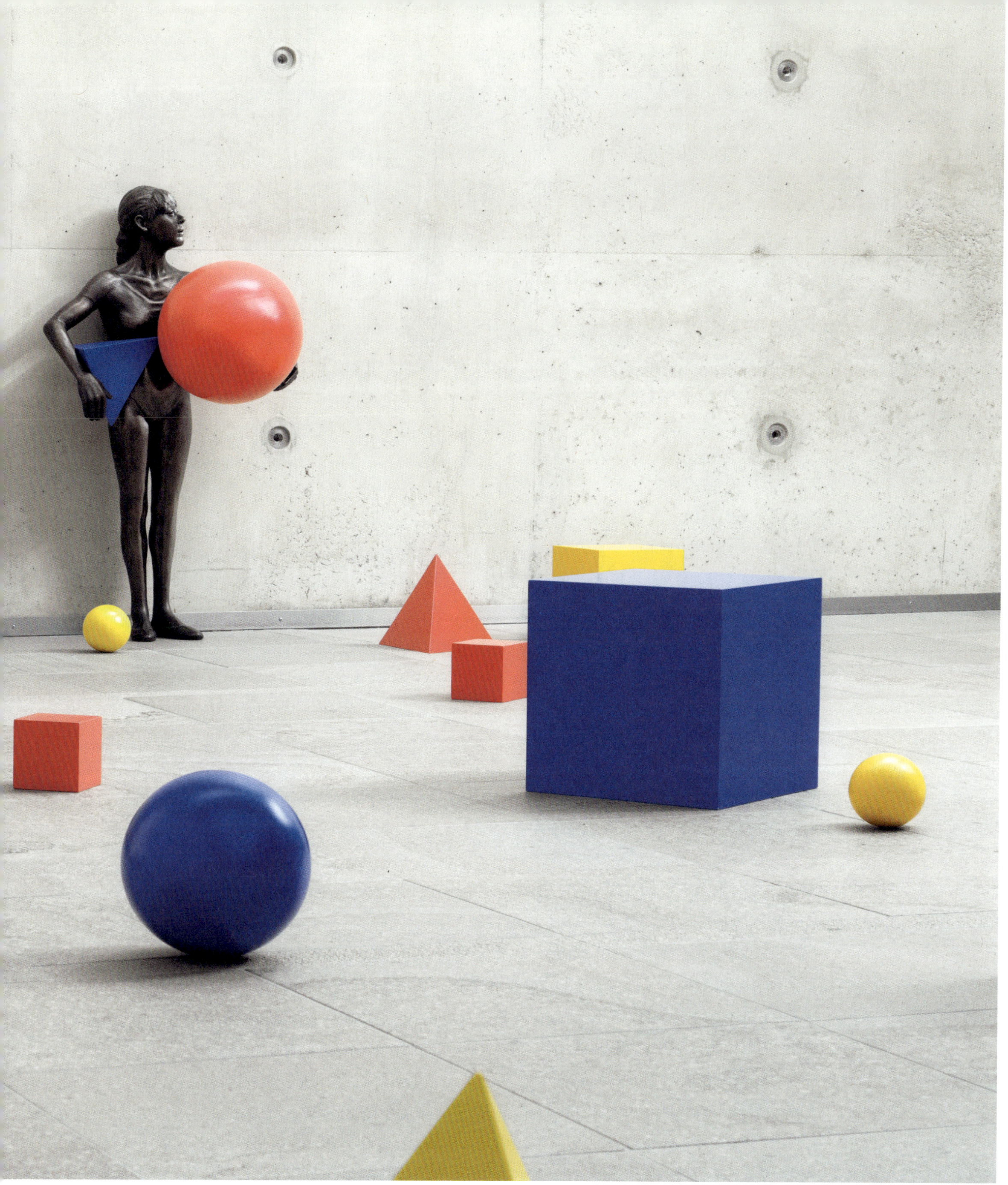

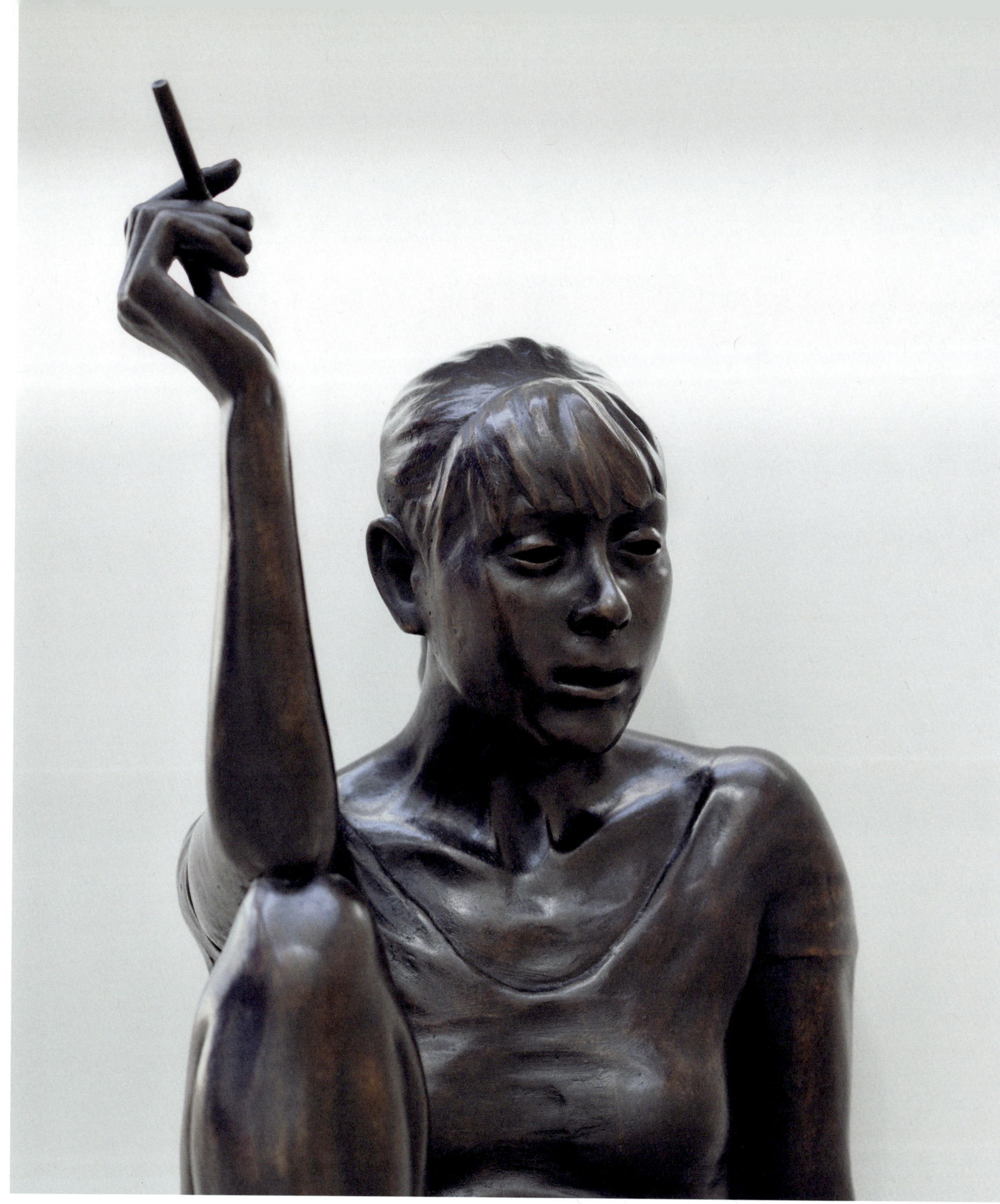

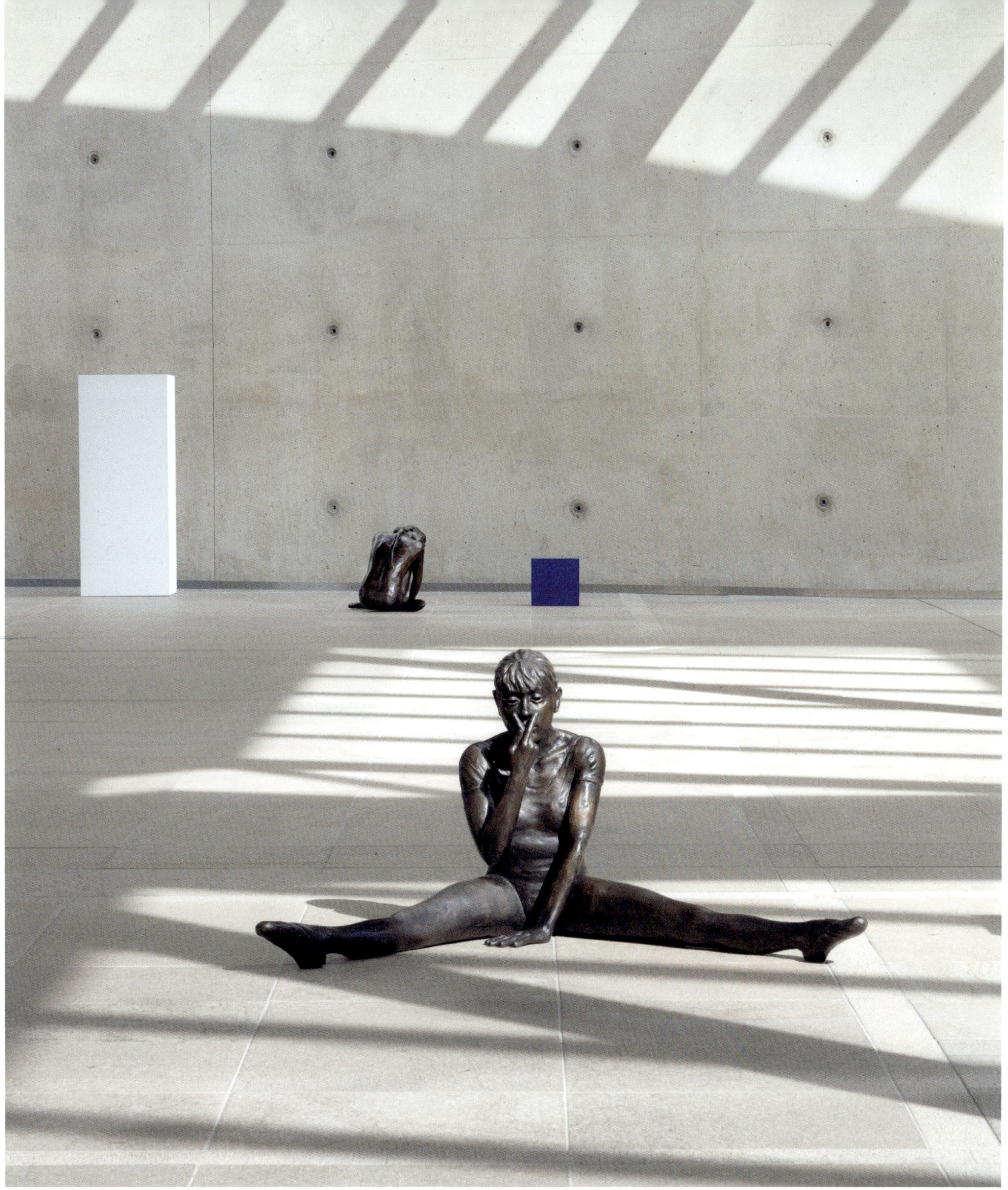

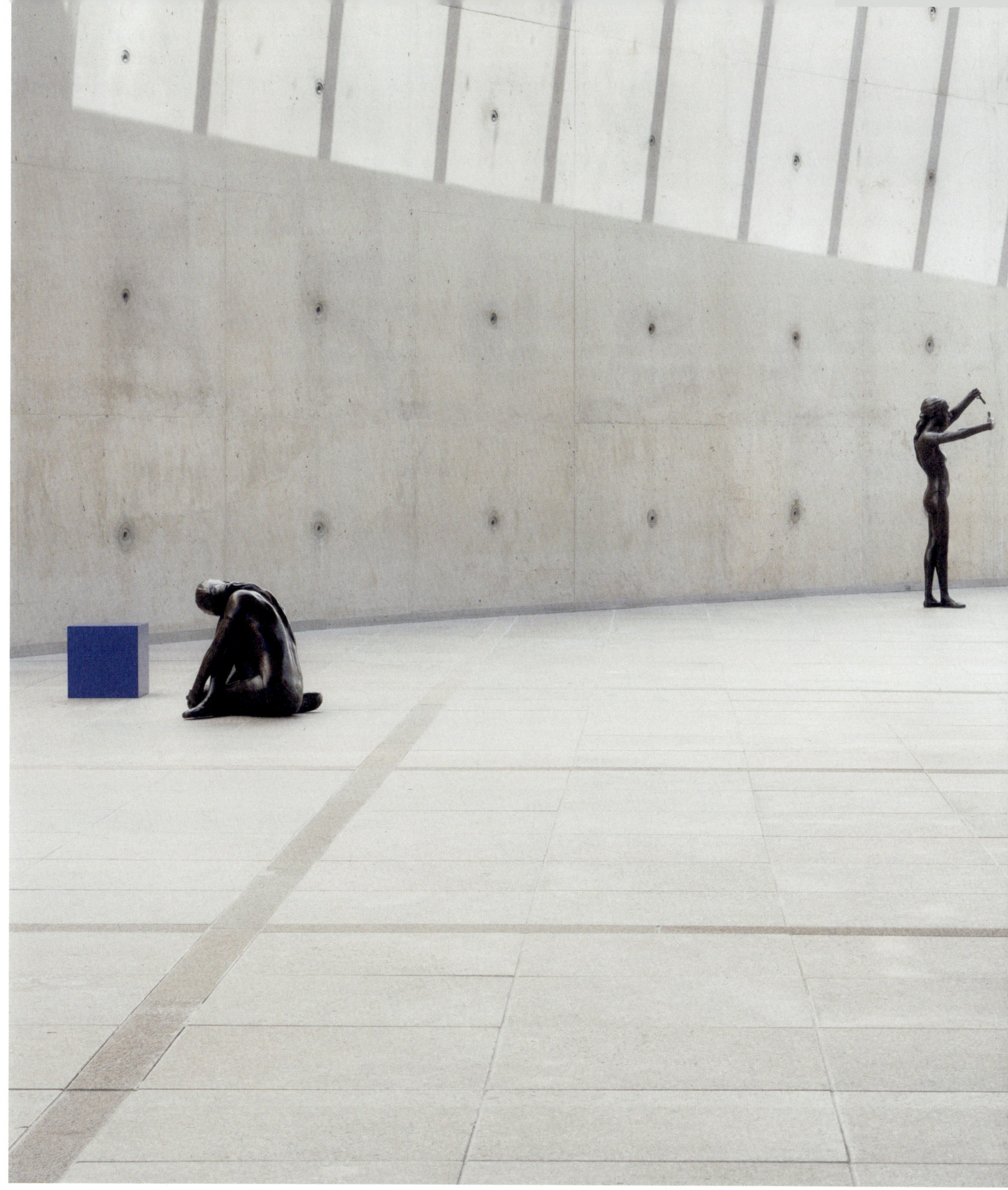

"RYAN GANDER'S BALLERINAS ARE WONDERFUL. HE SHOWS THAT THE BALLERINA CAN BE FREE, BY REMOVING HER FROM HER PEDESTAL."
PIPPA, 14 YEARS OLD

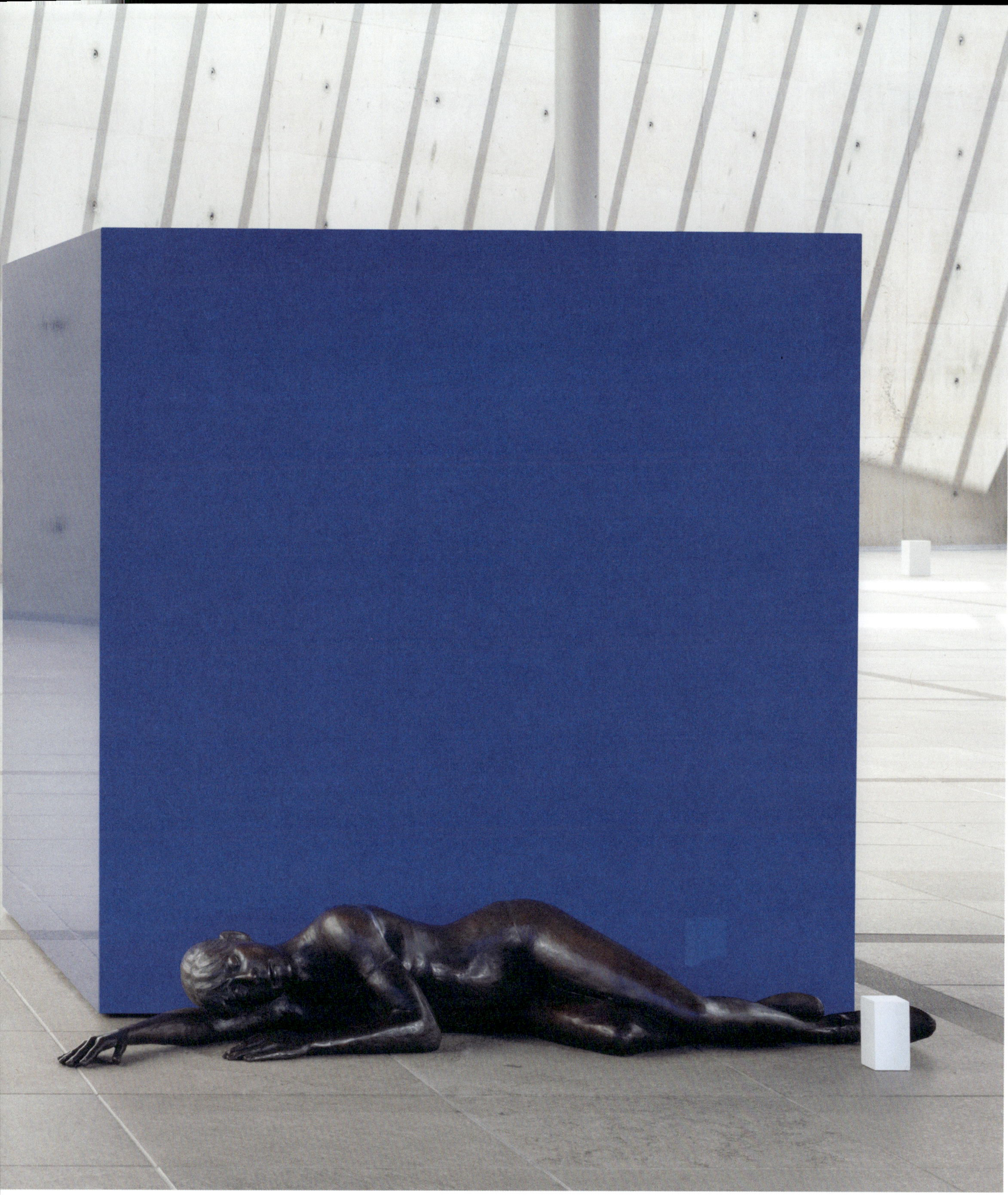

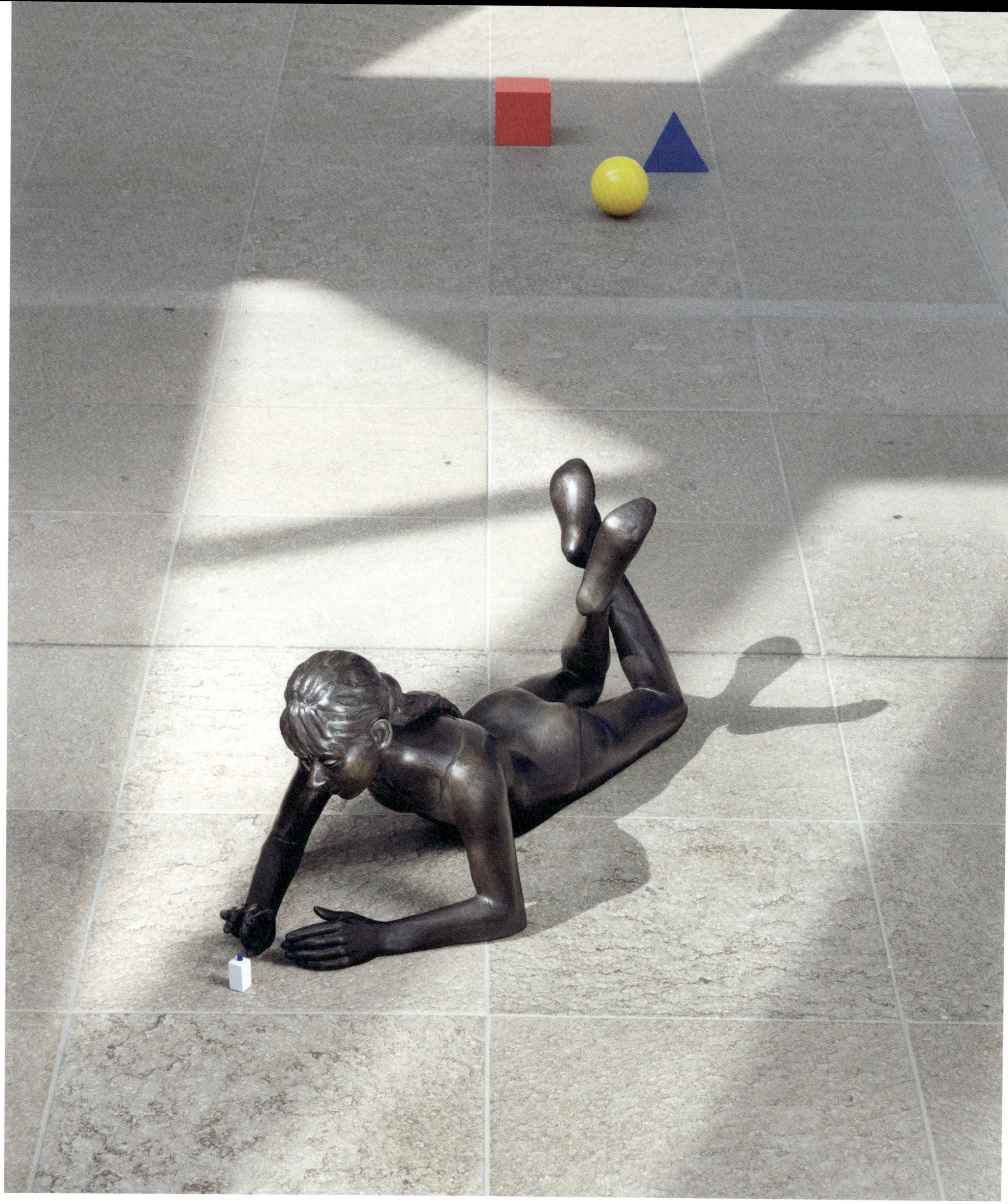

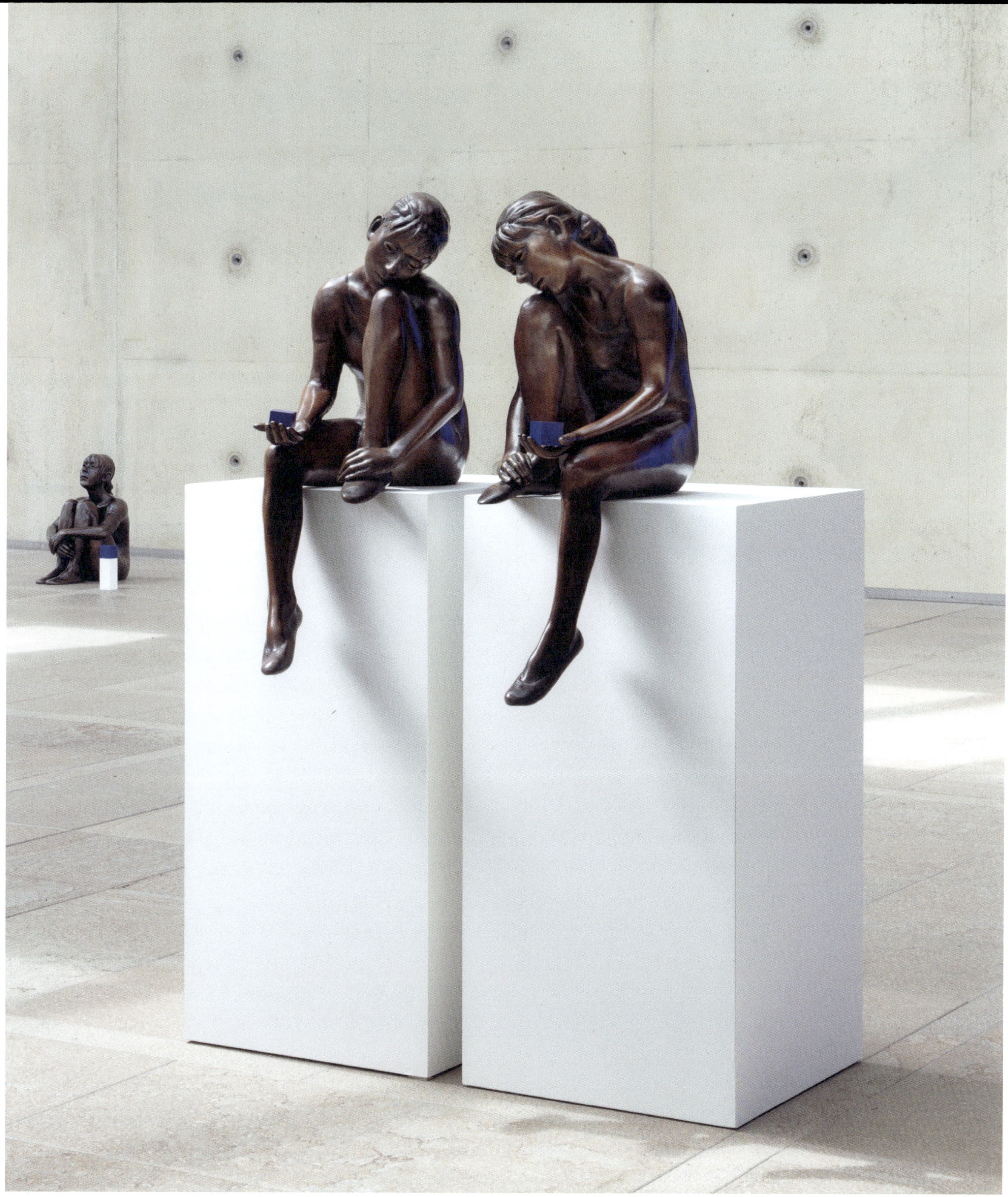

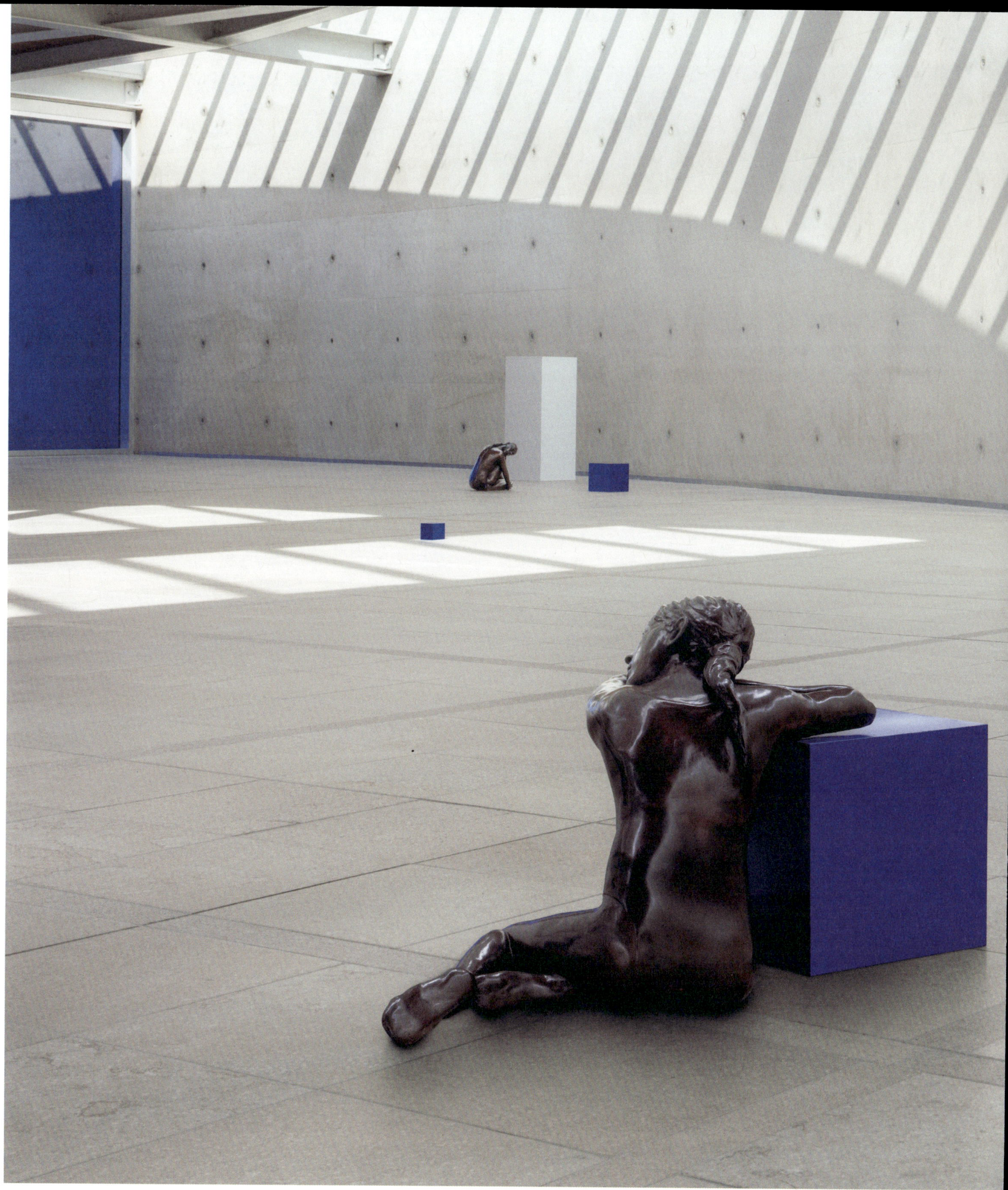

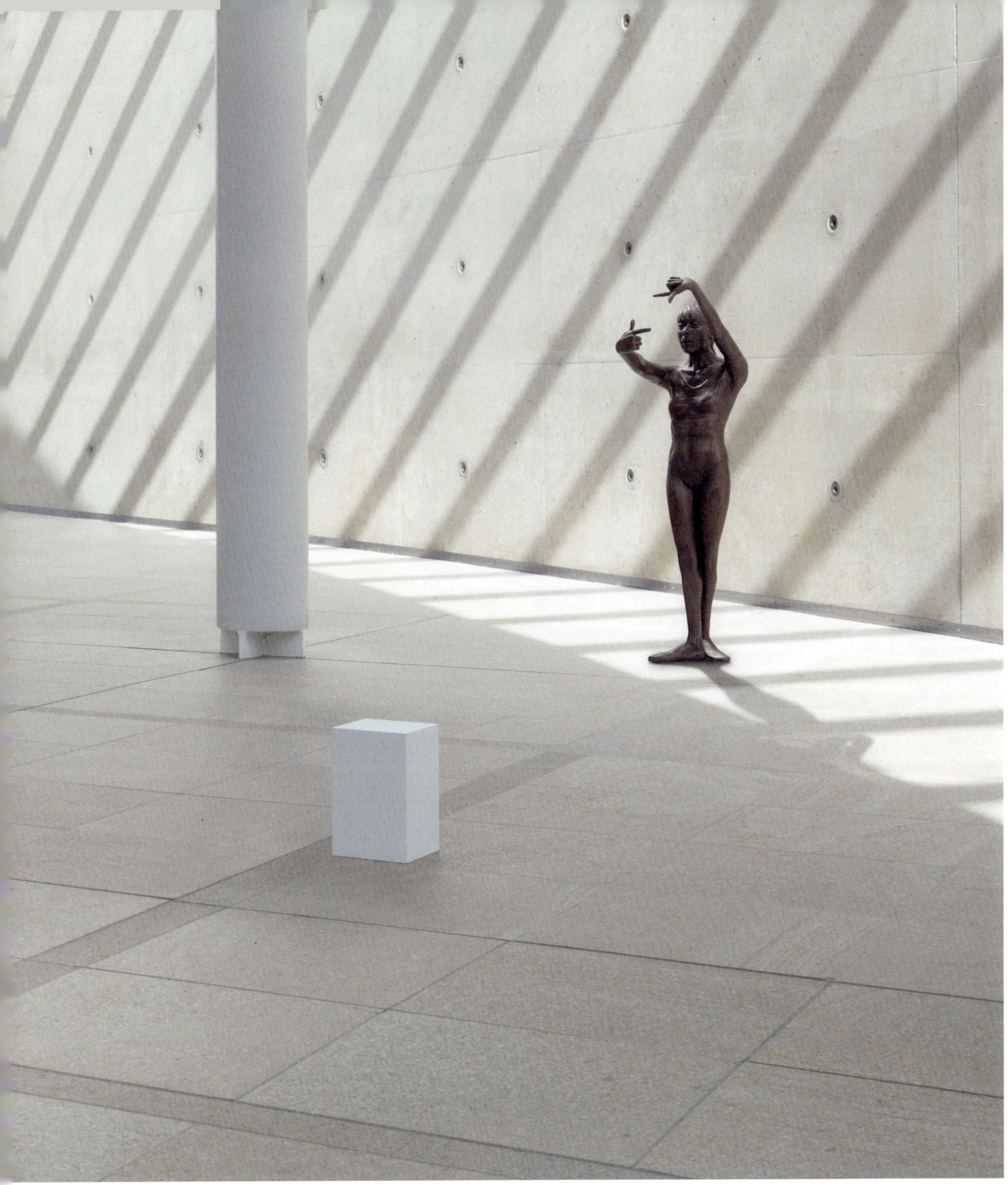

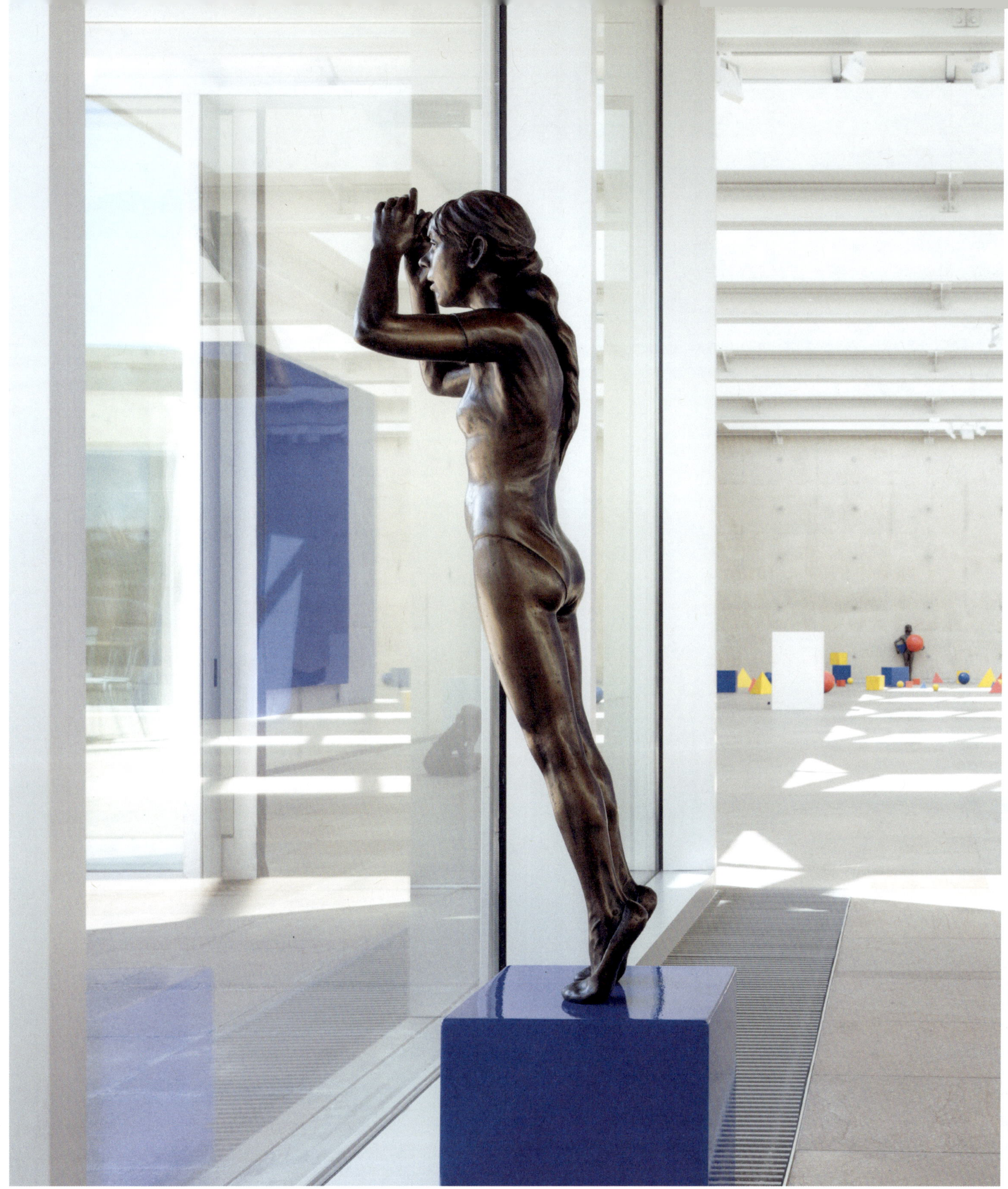

"EVERYONE THINKS THAT BALLERINAS ARE VERY LIVELY AND ALWAYS HAPPY, BUT IN THESE WORKS BY GANDER, YOU CAN SEE THAT IT CAN REALLY BE THE EXACT OPPOSITE AS WELL."
SANA, 14 YEARS OLD

Contents

A Pas de Deux: Ryan Gander in conversation with Edgar Degas

Brigitte Bloksma

Petite danseuse de quatorze ans (1880–81), the sculpture by Edgar Degas (1834–1917), occupies a unique position within western art history. When it was first shown in 1881 during the sixth exhibition staged by the impressionists in Paris, the press was shocked. A critic wrote: "She pushes her face forward with beastly impudence." The realistic representation of a young ballerina – without the usual idealization – caused great discomfort to the visitors. The sculpture was not cast in bronze, as was common at the time, but in wax. That material provided a precise, perfect rendering of the girl's skin. Furthermore, the little dancer had a wig of real hair on her head and wore a tutu and real ballet shoes, details that blurred the boundary between reality and art. Degas did not show the sublime beauty of the ballet, but a young girl caught between youth and adulthood, ambition and discipline.

Since 2008 the British artist Ryan Gander (1976) has been working on a conceptual series in which he reinterprets Degas's world-famous sculpture and places it in a contemporary context. Gander explores what the original little dancer signifies today, apart from her historical background. Dressed in a modern ballet suit instead of a classical tutu, Gander allows the ballerina to freely explore the museum room. He also places her in a new context and connects her to current ideas about time, identity and personality. Among other things, Gander does this by always accompanying his ballerina statues with a white plinth and a bright blue cube. These mysterious cubes offer space for interpretation and because of the different sizes the ballerinas seem to provide a changing dimension. For Gander blue is also the colour that symbolizes abstract ideas, as it often features in modern and contemporary art. Just think about *Blue Nudes* by Henri Matisse and Yves Klein's monochrome paintings in ultramarine blue.

Whereas Degas's work is a snapshot of a girl on the threshold of adulthood, Gander's sculptures depict imaginary timelines of the ballerina – alternative images of the future or reflections on what might have been. His approach is in line with the wider development of contemporary art, in which historical references function not simply as quotes, but as dynamic anchors for rewriting cultural narratives. In Gander's hands, Degas's fourteen-year-old dancer becomes a means to raise questions about themes of authority, the power of representation and the role of the art object as a narrator.

The *Ryan Gander X Edgar Degas – Pas de Deux* exhibition brings together twenty-one of his ballerina statues for the first time, and moreover in direct connection with Degas's iconic work. It is a meeting of past and present, between a girl observed from the nineteenth century and her contemporary interpretations. Together they form a poetic exploration of how the discourse and the ideas about artworks live on, change and also continue to appeal to us.

Since the beginning of his career Ryan Gander has developed an artistic practice that is difficult to pin down to a specific style or art discipline. His oeuvre includes sculpture, installation, photography, graphic design, performance and text, in which he systematically questions conventions around authorship, representation and exhibition form. Gander's work is often conceptual in nature; it is humorous, sensual and accessible. It invites viewers to interpret it without imposing itself. A fascination for the invisible, the untold and the potential of the imagination is always central in his work.

Against this backdrop, Gander's sculptural series of ballerinas is a layered and poetic exploration of Degas's *Petite danseuse*. Rather than creating a literal replica, Gander approaches the dancer as a figure that breaks away from her original, historical context. He literally frees her from her pedestal and places her in new situations and phases of life. His ballerinas rest, wander, dream and play – far from the stage. The sculptures are scenographic tableaus that transport viewers to the recognizable, everyday experiences of adolescents and young adults.

Gander's use of repetition, minimalism and sometimes subtle shifts in pose and context brings a contemporary interpretation of Degas's sculpture, while also transcending the original. By detaching the dancer from her original role as an object of the (male) gaze, he gives her a voice of her own. At the same time,

he reflects on the status of the artwork itself: how we conserve, reinterpret or once again even re-imagine images when they lose their original context. A good example of this is the work *As old as time itself, slept alone* (2016). This statue is of a girl who lies in a silent pose with her eyes closed, as if she is asleep. The physical vulnerability of her young body contrasts with the massive, bright blue cube next to her. In this composition, the girl seems not to want to be looked at, but to shut herself off from her surroundings in her dreams. In this way, Gander overturns the historical power relationship of Degas's sculpture: from object of the gaze to a subject in reflection.

Another work, *Epiphany...learnt through hardship* (2012), shows the little dancer seated, with her legs drawn up and her head resting on her knees. Here the theatrical tension of Degas's stage posture has disappeared completely; the figure appears introverted, vulnerable and absent from the world. Moreover, she is in the same pose as the model in the famous photograph *Nude* (1936) by Edward Weston (1886–1958), a pioneer of modern photography. In the work *I don't blame you, or, When we made love you used to cry and I love you like the stars above and I'll love you till I die* (2008), Gander again changes the perspective. He depicts the girl seated with a cigarette in her hand. A relaxed pose that seems almost meditative, as if she is consciously withdrawing from the spectacle that was once her *raison d'être*.

In Gander's most recent work, *Waiting for timefall, or, Living in a time where everything is possible, but nothing can happen* (2025), the dancer is no longer the sole object of reflection; she is integrated into a larger, almost cosmic perspective. The work shows the ballerina against the background of a large blue surface, in a moment of stillness, as if waiting for something beyond her reach – which refers to the idea of 'waiting' as an active state of being. This image evokes the tension between the desire for control over the concept of time and its inevitable progression.

By bringing together Gander's ballerina statues in one exhibition, it becomes clear how his series has developed over a period of

fifteen years into a visual novel: each work is a scene, a moment or a memory from a life that does not fit into one time or space. The ballerina is therefore no longer an icon, but a human figure with insecurities, doubts and dreams that are recognizable to everyone.

Gander's tilting of the perspective in Degas's original work is continued in the concept of the exhibition. The way in which the sculptures are placed in the space, and in particular the way in which viewers move towards them, is a voyage of discovery. As visitors, you are challenged to be part of a choreography where past and present come together. It is as if you are in a dream world, where the familiar forms of reality fade away and a sense of wonder arises – comparable to *Alice in Wonderland*, where everything moves and changes, but at the same time appears to be real. For example, in the work *Local and global reaching out, or, And sailed back over a year, And in and out of weeks, And through a day* (2017), Gander's ballerina crawls out of a small white pedestal which is placed in a large white pedestal. This large pedestal transforms the exhibition space and shifts the viewer's perspective. What is more, something unexpected happens: the pedestal shifts the focus of the work from a simple object in space to an interaction of the viewers with the work itself. The height and position of the pedestal almost forces the viewer to go inside and become part of the artwork.

The exhibition invites viewers not only to be present as spectators, but as active participants who, through their way of looking and moving, help shape the experience. This interaction makes the experience of the exhibition intimate and constantly in motion. Degas's sculpture *Petite danseuse de quatorze ans*, which is normally shown as the showpiece in an open museum space, is hidden in a large blue cube. At first glance, it seems inaccessible; it is a mystery that only unfolds for the curious viewers. The cube functions as a space for silence and introspection, in which Degas's ballerina invites viewers to reflect on their own perception of the here and now. What is often experienced as fixed in the traditional museum space – the image as an object of admiration – is changed here into a moment of personal interaction.

The dialogue in this exhibition of a world-famous, nineteenth-century girl, observed for centuries, and her contemporary echoes is above all an exploration of the power of visual art to transform our understanding of time and space.

The idea for the exhibition arose three years ago during a conversation with the art collector Jack Bakker. He encouraged me to stage this exhibition. I would like to thank him and all the other private individuals and museum lenders from the Netherlands, Germany, Switzerland, England and Japan who so generously lent their work by Ryan Gander to Museum Beelden aan Zee. I would also like to thank Museum Boijmans Van Beuningen for the generous loan of Petite danseuse de quatorze ans (1880–81) by Edgar Degas and the good cooperation in the run-up to the exhibition. I would also like to thank Sandra Kisters, director of Collections at Museum Boijmans Van Beuningen, the writer Lydia Figes and the fourteen-year-olds for their contribution to this catalogue.

The exhibition and this catalogue could not have come about without the generous financial support of the VriendenLoterij, the Don Quixote Foundation, the LIDA Fonds, the Blockbusterfonds, Gemeente Den Haag, Stichting Retourschip, Molsbergen Development, Stichting Zabawas, Mondriaan Fonds and private donors. This project was made possible by a contribution from the Zadelhoff Cultuur Fonds. I'd also like to thank Ryan Gander Studio, Lisson Gallery, Annet Gelink Gallery, TARO NASU Gallery, Esther Schipper, exhibition designer Magali Snelder, catalogue designer Linda van Deursen, photographer Studio Gerrit Schreurs and the team at Museum Beelden aan Zee for the fantastic collaboration.

To Ryan Gander, finally; your work gives every visitor the opportunity to be part of a performance that, like the ballerina, places itself in a new time and space with every turn and movement. Thank you for the inspiring journey.

Brigitte Bloksma
Director Museum Beelden aan Zee,
Curator Ryan Gander X Edgar Degas – Pas de Deux

Literature list

Bishop, C. (2012) I Artificial Hells: Participatory Art and the Politics of Spectatorship. Verso.

Czestochowski, J. and Pingeot, A. (2002) Degas Sculptures I The Torch Press and International Arts.

Gander, R. (undated) I Sculpture Works. https://ryanganderarchive.com

Jones, A. (2012) I Seeing Differently: A History and Theory of Identification and the Visual Arts. Routledge.

Kendall, R. (1998) I Degas and the Little Dancer. Yale University Press.

Nochlin, L. (1994) I Representing Women. Thames & Hudson.

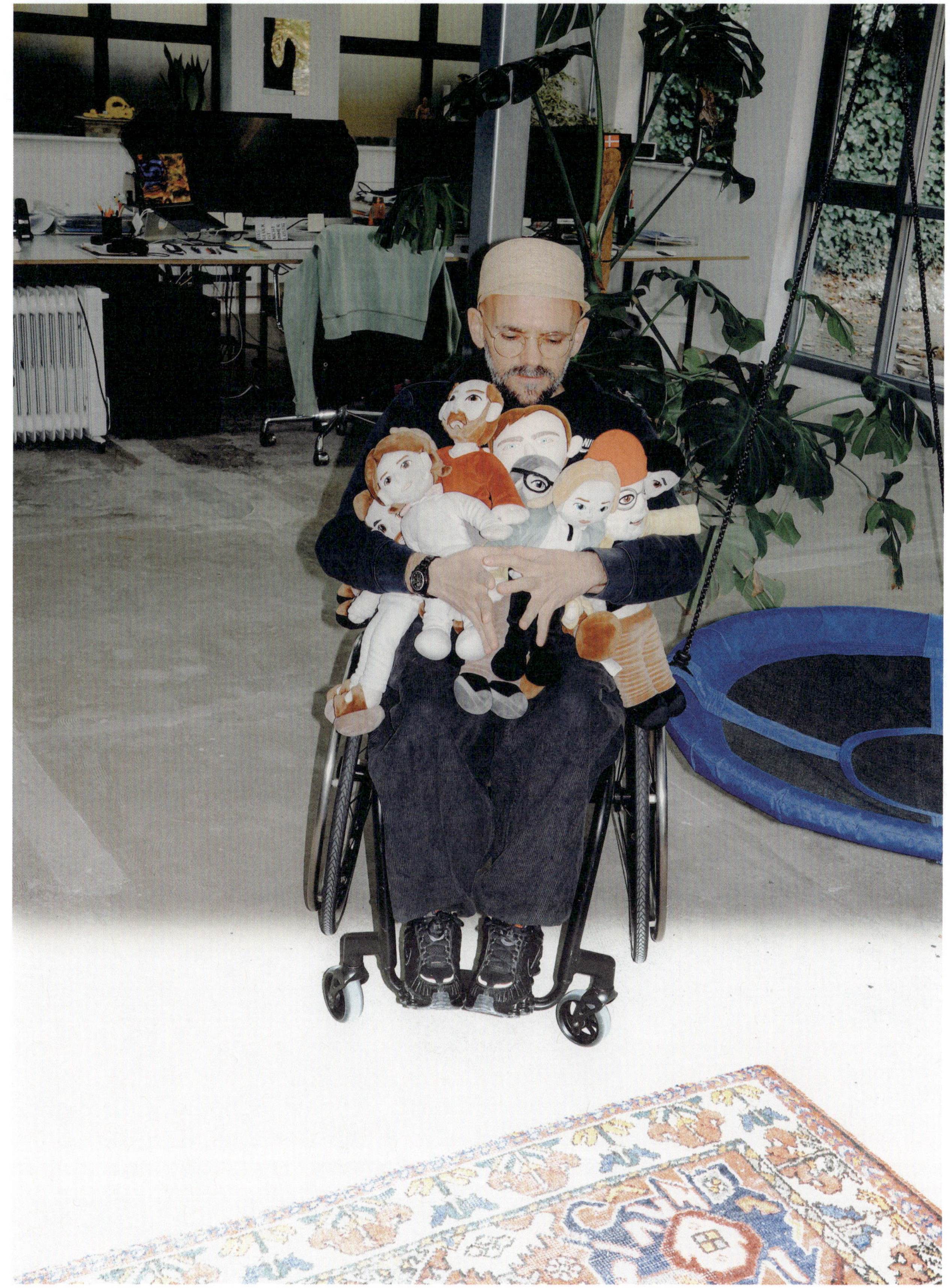

The politics of spectatorship: an interview with Ryan Gander

Lydia Figes

Ryan Gander OBE RA*, was born in Chester in the northwest of England in 1976. Now based in rural Suffolk on the east coast of the UK, where he runs his busy studio out of a converted, high-ceilinged sports hall, he is considered one of Britain's foremost contemporary artists. Since the early 2000s, he has exhibited widely and internationally, building complex and versatile bodies of work that span many mediums: sculpture, installation, animatronics, performance, design, and publications. Often recognisable for their distinctive humour, Gander's work – despite the breadth of mediums and materials – commonly conveys a soft irreverence, crypticism and self-referentiality. Gander typically pursues ideas over aesthetics, and his conceptually-led art demands a cognitive exercise from those who behold it. *"Going to a gallery is like taking your imagination to the gym"* is one of his most memorable mantras.

Studying photography and fine art, first at the Manchester Metropolitan University (1999), followed by the Jan van Eyck Academie, Maastricht (2000), Gander finished his studies at Amsterdam's Rijksakademie van Beeldende Kunsten (2002). He was awarded an OBE (Officer of the Order of the British Empire) in 2017, and elected a Royal Academician in 2022. Gander's career has taken him to all corners of the world. Yet his humble beginnings in middle England during Thatcher's era instilled in him a particular way of perceiving his surroundings – one which sets him apart from artworld elitism. The son of a Vauxhall car engineer and a school teacher, Gander describes his upbringing as ordinary and suburban. Immersion in art history was not part of his daily life as a child or adolescent. *"The place I grew up in was traditionally working class, yet aspirational"* he explains. *"My parents worked all the time, and we didn't have things like books, musical instruments, or art in the house."* He also explains that much of his early life was spent in hospital, meaning he was socialised around adults rather than children. In spite of (or conversely, because of) these creative limitations, Gander has proven to be an astute observer of contemporary life. And it is this quality that draws him closer to the historic figure of Edgar Degas (1834–1917), a key figure in late nineteenth-century art, who created his sculpture <u>Petite danseuse de quatorze ans</u> (<u>Little Dancer Aged Fourteen</u>) in 1881.

Over a century later, Gander delves back into art history to reimagine Degas's ballerina. By doing so, he creates something distinctly contemporary, albeit with a Ganderesque twist. The exhibition <u>Ryan Gander X Edgar Degas – Pas de Deux</u> offers more than an artistic homage to Degas. It provides a tongue-in-cheek, visual riddle, one bringing into question the intricacies of spectatorship itself. Playing upon the theme of ballet and the titular 'pas de deux', the artist proposes a dialogue (or dance) with Degas's ballerina, who in this instance, has been given permission to escape her pedestal and roam around the gallery with apparent free will. As a consequence, we – the audience – become aware of how we move within the gallery space, how we engage with the work, and in return, how she engages with us.

"The first time I saw a Degas was at Pittsburgh's Carnegie Museum, whilst installing my work in the Carnegie International." Gander tells me as we sit in the vast, minimalist space of his Suffolk studio. *"It was eerily quiet at the museum as I was installing a work after the museum had closed to the public."* In a neighbouring gallery, Degas ballerina stood alone in the centre of the dimly-lit room. *"The lights were half on and there was no security around. It was just me and the sculpture. It felt a bit creepy being in the museum because it was closed. But every time I'd walk past her, it felt like she was observing me. I'd raise my head and eyebrows at the sculpture – as if to say hello."* The regularity of walking past the solitary sculpture sparked his interest. *"All of a sudden she became very familiar. The relationship became a casual one, more so than if I had been a normal spectator visiting the museum. It dawned on me that she was also a spectator – just like me."*

For Gander, the familial dynamic with Degas's sculpture prompted deeper reflection about art spectatorship. Traditionally speaking, the art object is considered to be a passive entity that is contained within the gallery or museum walls. In post-structuralist theory, we might consider the artwork to be interpretively open; its meaning is unfixed and unstable. Equally, it can defy or even resist the strictures of the institution itself. Taking this concept one step further, Gander's reinterpretation of the Degas ballerina imbues the artwork with agency. And by doing so, he flips the script of spectatorship; the binary of active spectator and passive art object is inverted. *"We refer to an equation between the institution, art work and spectator that is completely mixed up. So I tried to change the position and renegotiate those three things. I turned the Degas sculpture into a spectator rather than a sculpture."*

Gander deploys abstract components — white plinths and blue cubes — to symbolise the nexus of spectatorship in the museum context. *"The white plinth represents the institution, the weight and history of art, or even the pomp and circumstance of it all compounded with the entanglement of cultural, historical baggage"* Gander explains. *"The cube symbolises contemporary art. It's simple and eloquent, evoking modernism and the Bauhaus cube. Lastly, the Degas bronze sculpture is the red herring. You initially think that the sculpture could be a historical artwork. But really it's a signifier of the spectator."*

But for Gander, spectatorship isn't neutral. The act of looking at art within the museum is a behaviour determined by taste, education and even class. Reflecting the real responses of many museum visitors, Gander's ballerina sometimes looks distracted, despondent — even bored. For the artist, this reflects the experience of many museum visitors, especially in the UK where art historical education is limited and the enjoyment of going to a museum is quite often contingent upon social background and one's level of education. *"Playing with the sculpture in this way got me thinking about my mum,"* Gander says. *"She isn't a particularly learned person when it comes to art and visual culture. She isn't used to looking at art or going to a museum. For her, and many people from her sort of class background in Britain, there's a stigma when going into a museum. They feel uncomfortable, and like they don't belong there. They probably fear they aren't academic enough to deal with what's happening in a museum."*

"When my mum goes to a museum, she will traditionally sit on a bench in the middle of the gallery. She'll observe an artwork, but in reality, she's not looking at the art" Gander confesses. *"She's more interested in observing the people, who are looking at the art. But I have this in common with her: I'm interested in observing the sociology and spectatorship around the art, often more than looking at the art itself. Because really, art only becomes art when somebody is looking at it. The proof that an artwork is alive is that people are looking at it."*

From the artist's perspective, his recreation of Degas's ballerina communicates something more honest about the human condition. *"She's closer to how people really behave in museums,"* Gander insists. *"She reminds me of those groups of school children in the gallery."* Indeed, the fact that the ballerina is still a child, on the threshold of adulthood is key here. *"There's an innocence and naivete to the figure. I associate her age with that moment in early adolescence when people are their most creative. Young adolescents don't read work with any stigma, which means they can have more interesting responses to art. They'll interpret art with honesty, perhaps saying things that adults wouldn't dare say because it's too obvious."* In short, what is revealed is that spectatorship is partly performative and socially scripted.

In ironic contrast, when Degas's original ballerina — sculpted in wax rather than bronze — was first exhibited in Paris at the Sixth Impressionist Exhibition in 1881, it scandalised onlookers and was considered anything but innocent. There are several reasons for this. Firstly, the sculpture had been fabricated in highly unconventional materials. Degas's lifelike wax figure adorned in real clothing (a fabric tutu and a wig with actual hair) was considered unrefined and disturbing, diverging from traditional sculptural renderings. But the lack of refinement was also due to the subject matter. At the time, ballet dancers were perceived as being synonymous to sex workers. Often disparagingly referred to as the 'petits rats' for their associations with poverty and prostitution, young ballerinas were at the mercy of their lustful and powerful patrons. The model employed by Degas, Marie van Goethem, was a real ballerina in training, who was from a working-class background and whom the artist first met in 1878, using her as a model for many of his drawings and paintings.

But the realism, posture and countenance of Degas's ballerina also provoked audiences. The ballerina's air of defiance and impertinence conveyed through her upturned chin was deemed to be improper for such a sordid subject matter. It was unanimously agreed by critics that she was ugly, with one critic describing the sculpture as *"simply hideous"*, and another noting that she resembled a medical specimen, an impression heightened by the fact that Degas displayed her in a glass vitrine. Known only as a painter until the early 1880s, this was the first occasion in which Degas publicly exhibited sculpture. But his creation was ridiculed by large swathes of his contemporaries. Only after Degas's death in 1917, when his family organised for many of his wax sculptures to be cast in bronze, was the sculpture brought back to life and monumentalised in the more serious, art historical material of bronze. There are now at least 29 bronze casts of Degas's ballerina all around the world. Like Gander's ballerina, the original creation has taken on a life and significance of its own.

Prior to his first encounter with Degas's sculpture, Gander knew he always wanted to experiment with bronze casting. Materially speaking, bronze represents the establishment and power, evoking antiquity and equestrian statues. It symbolises the weight and seriousness of history. Therefore, it is rife with opportunities to playfully subvert the subject of sculpture and art history. *"Because of the kind of neo-conceptual way that I make work, I knew that I couldn't make my own sculpture"* Gander states. *"I'd need to source something rooted in history and stories. There had to be a reason to cast something in bronze. I can't justify making a work that is too cognitively simple, and the material has to speak to that complexity."* Degas's divisive ballerina proved to be the perfect springboard, one which Gander continues to return to each year — nearly two decades later. *"The viewer needs to be challenged by the work, to the point where maybe they get lost in it. Good art starts in one place and ends in a million places"* the artist adds. *"If it only has one interpretation, art is purely communication — it has to offer more than that."*

So why has Gander repeatedly returned to this body of work? What is it about Degas's ballerina that continues to intrigue? Since 2008, the artist has reimagined and restaged the ballerina in a multitude of different positions, initially using his ex-wife as a model for the casting, before working with professional dancers to pose in different positions, whom he would photograph to later consider the variety of postures. Gander's series forms part of a larger narrative, one unfolding slowly and intermittently over the decades. In early renditions, such as <u>I don't blame you, or, When we made love...</u> (2008), <u>Tight and formless thinking...</u>

(2010) and Bleak Endings and Eve Online, or, Ryandóttir (2013) she appears to be adjusting to the newfound freedom from her plinth. While in later versions, such as As old as time itself, slept alone (2016), she reclines on the gallery floor, apparently exhausted by the conditions of her freedom within the museum.

The exhibition in Museum Beelden aan Zee showcasing twenty-one out of twenty-nine ballerinas is crucially the first time that nearly the entire body of work is assembled in one place. This is significant, because as Gander explains, storytelling has always been behind the conception of the work, and how he imagines the ballerina might behave if she was liberated from her plinth. *"I returned to this subject again and again because it's almost like a cartoon strip. Each one is a part of a wider story and character arc. However, they weren't made in the correct order of that story, so in that sense, the story is non-linear."*

Gander gives his ballerina a life of her own. But rather than simply appropriating Degas's ballerina, he creates his own dance with the audience, to probe into our relationship with the art object and the museum containing it. *"It's all part of an attempt to domesticate the institution, or simply to make the institution more casual. These works are exercises in deinstitutionalising the institution."*

* OBE: Officer of the Order of the British Empire
RA: Member of the Royal Academy of Arts

Not just one sculpture, but many: Degas's little dancer

Sandra Kisters

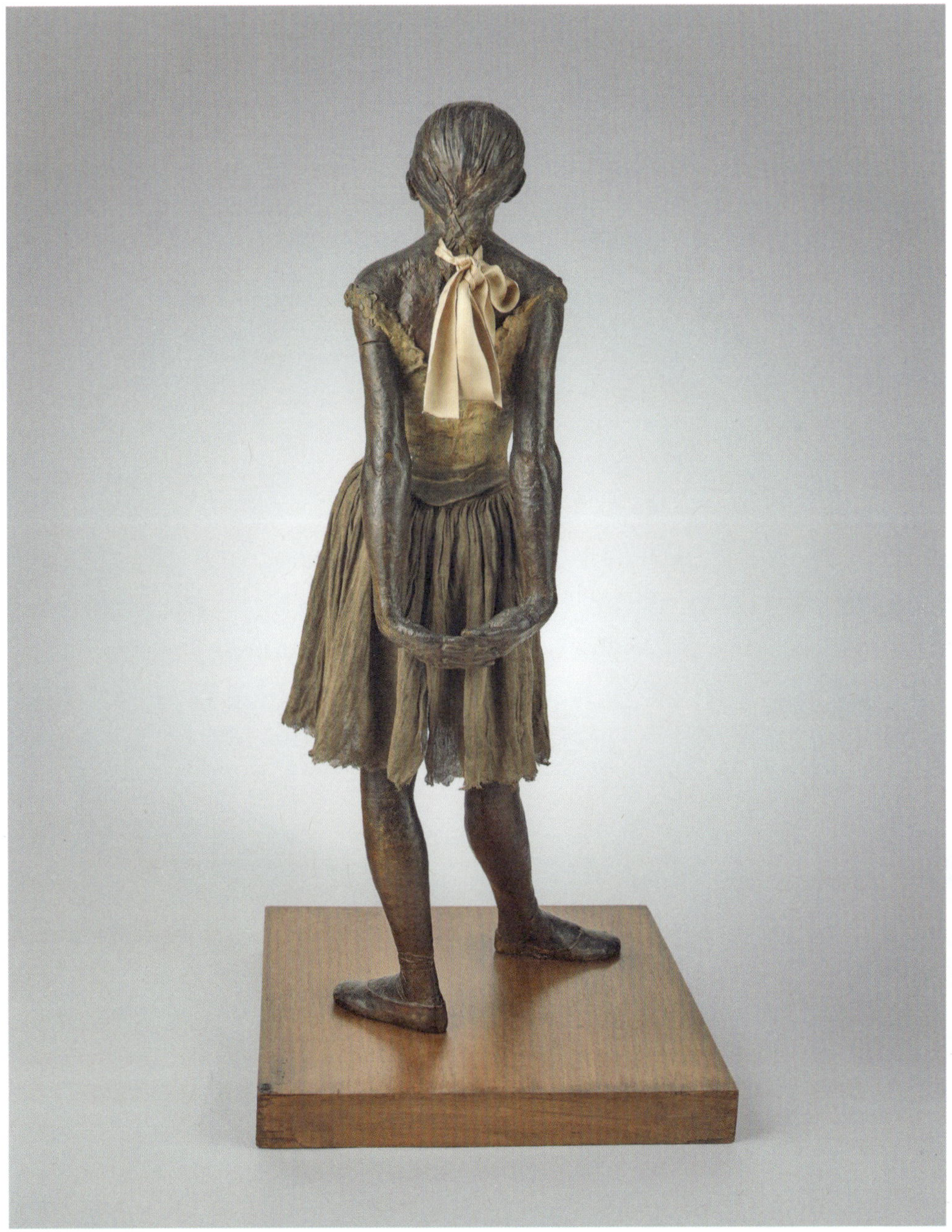

Who doesn't know her? The little fourteen-year-old dancer who's a little bored, her head tilted back slightly, and her hands behind her back, seems to be waiting for directions from the choreographer or a telling-off from the dance instructor. She can be seen in various international museums, always in a slightly different tutu, although not always with a bow in her hair or wearing real ballet slippers. Museum Boijmans Van Beuningen in Rotterdam also has a bronze cast in its collection [fig. 1]. The statue was purchased at the Rondom Rodin exhibition, which was staged in the Stedelijk Museum Amsterdam in 1939.[1] Immediately afterwards it was to be seen in the annual Christmas exhibition in Museum Boymans, as the museum was still called at that time, together with Pierre de Wissant (one of the figures from the Burghers of Calais) (1885–86) by Auguste Rodin (1840–1917), which had also been acquired at the exhibition at the Stedelijk. A journalist from the Rotterdamsch Nieuwsblad wrote about the two sculptures enthusiastically and specifically about the little dancer: "[...] first of all people will be inclined to take pleasure from the arrogant attitude of this little ballet rat, who's actually just a mouse."[2] Since then she has almost always been on display, although she is occasionally loaned to another museum, like now in 2025 to Museum Beelden aan Zee for the Ryan Gander X Edgar Degas – Pas de Deux exhibition.

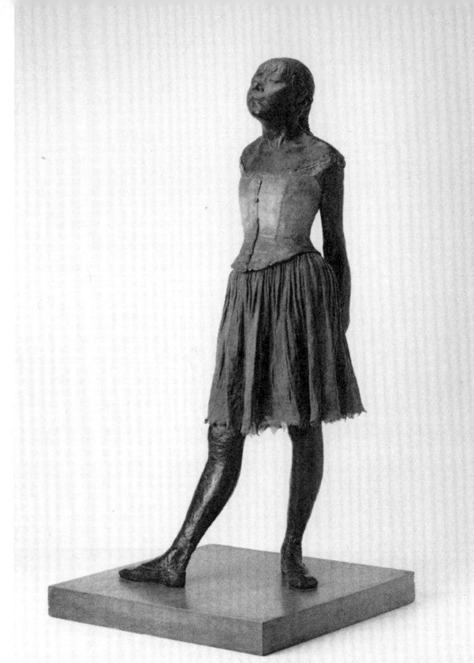

fig 1. Edgar Degas, Petite danseuse de quatorze ans, 1880–81 (1922), bronze and textile, 98 × 49 × 50 cm, collection Museum Boijmans Van Beuningen, Rotterdam.

With its height of 98 centimetres the statue is around two-thirds of the size of the model, fourteen year-old Marie Geneviève van Goethem (1865– after 1922), who when she posed for the sculpture, was training to be a ballet dancer at the Opéra in Paris, like her sister Charlotte.[3] In 1882 she was dismissed, probably because she had become the talk of the town due to immoral behaviour.[4] The two sisters posed for Edgar Degas (1834–1917) several times. The little dancer is noticeably larger than the other sculptures we know of by Degas. They are usually smaller studies of female dancers, horses or women bathing [figs. 2, 3]. In many respects the little dancer is an exceptional case. It is the only sculpture that Degas ever exhibited, differs in size and material from the other sculptures he made, and has become one of the most famous sculptures in the world. Yet the sculpture does not stand alone.

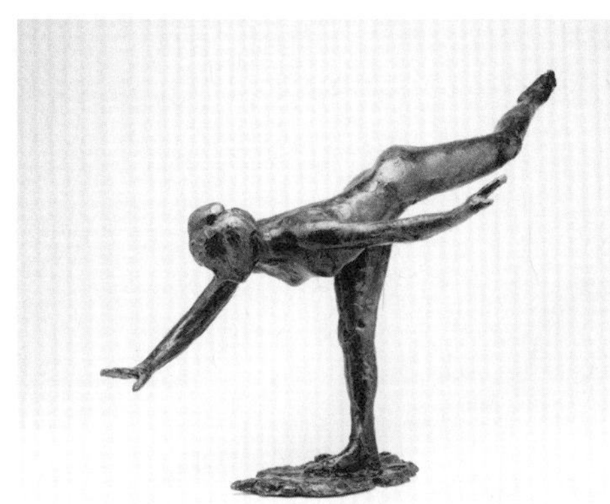

fig 2. Edgar Degas, Grande Arabesque, troisième temps (Grande Arabesque, third position), ca. 1885–1890, bronze, à cire perdue, 39 × 56 × 11.8 cm, collection Museum Boijmans Van Beuningen, Rotterdam.

Degas is well-known from his many representations of ballet dancers. Although at first glance they seem to be too sweet for modern viewers, because of the flimsy tutus and the colourful, impressionist execution in pastel chalk, they are in line with the realistic focus within his oeuvre. Think of the horse races depicted by Degas, tired washerwomen, drunken people in a pub, and the dancers of the Paris Opéra, who certainly did not have a spotless reputation at the end of the nineteenth century.

The dancers were often of humble origins and were under pressure to please the male, well-to-do visitors. They were associated with prostitution and because of their often poor backgrounds were disparagingly called 'rats', the young little dancers in particular.[5] All in all, Degas did not so much depict the ballet performances, but rather the dancers waiting in the wings, dancers doing exercises or putting on pointe shoes, tired or bored, and the lessons in the ballet studio. He always focused on the physical exertion, the movements and the correct postures. He began drawing and painting dancers in the late 1860s in idiosyncratic compositions that betray the influence of photography, such as The Orchestra of the Opéra from 1870. The subject of life in the opera, of dancers and musicians, would continue to fascinate him in the decades that followed.

The 1881 exhibition

From the beginning, from 1874 onwards, Degas took part in the exhibitions staged by a group of like-minded artists, because the official Paris Salon often refused to display their works. This group, the Société anonyme des artistes peintres, sculpteurs et graveurs, later became known as the impressionists. They staged eight exhibitions in total. Those exhibitions featured a wide range of artworks, and certainly not everything fell under the heading of what we would today call impressionist. Although the work by the best-known participants: Camille Pissarro (1830–1903), Paul Cézanne (1839–1906), Claude Monet (1840–1926), Berthe Morisot (1841–1895), Alfred Sisley (1839–1899) and Degas, can be described as such. Degas frequently exhibited drawings, paintings and prints of female ballet dancers, including

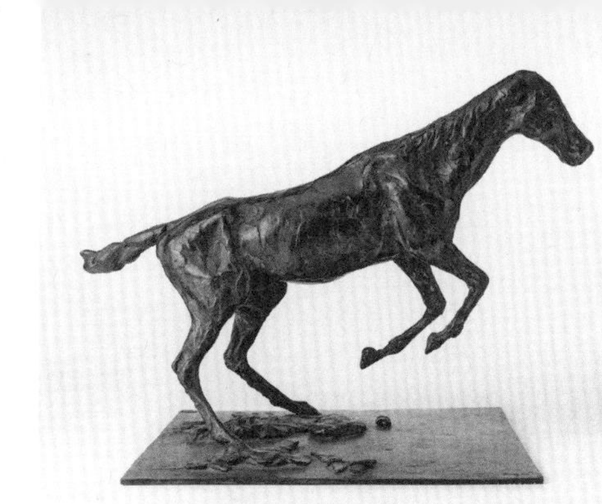

fig 3. Edgar Degas, Horse taking an obstacle, 1881–1890, bronze, à cire perdue, 29 × 41.5 × 24 cm, collection Museum Boijmans Van Beuningen, Rotterdam.

the painting The Dancing Class (1870) at the first exhibition in 1874 [fig. 4].[6]

Degas showed a sculpture for the first and only time in the sixth exhibition by the impressionists in 1881: a wax figure of a little dancer, a girl of fourteen, in a real bodice and a tulle skirt. She was wearing real ballet slippers, and a wig of human hair, made by the doll maker Mme Cusset. Her little body and slippers were covered with a layer of wax. Her plait was tied with a silk ribbon. The simple, square pedestal was made of wood.[7] The material used cause the greatest fuss. Instead of terracotta, plaster, marble or stone, he used wax, a material which was usually used for anatomical models. This realism was not seen as a skilful presentation of sculpture by the Parisian Académie des Beaux Arts. Moreover, it was never used as the final result, but artists first presented completed images in plaster, before they were executed in another material such as bronze. The critic Jules Claritie (1840–1913) wrote about it derogatory: "There wasn't enough colour. They must have used wax, or plaster or bronze. Good God, what are we going to see! Impressionist sculptures."[8] Displaying the sculpture in a glass case also caused negative reactions, because it called to mind anthropological presentations or relics which were also often exhibited in showcases.[9] The fact that the sculpture was not idealized and did not conform to the classical proportions, were also subjects of criticism. It was even suggested that the young little dancer was sexually active, such as by the art critic Charles Ephrussi (1849–1905): "the Opera rat in her modern form, learning her craft, with all her disposition and stock of bad instincts and licentious inclinations", "the intimate allures and profession of the individual."[10] By contrast, the symbolist writer Joris-Karl Huysmans (1848–1907) praised its modernity: "The terrible realism of this statuette makes the public distinctly uneasy, all its ideas about sculpture, about cold lifeless whiteness ... are demolished. [...] this statuette is the only truly modern attempt I know in sculpture."[11]

After the devastating reactions, Degas decided to no longer exhibit his sculptures, but he continued to work on them in the privacy of his studio. Many a visitor, among them the American

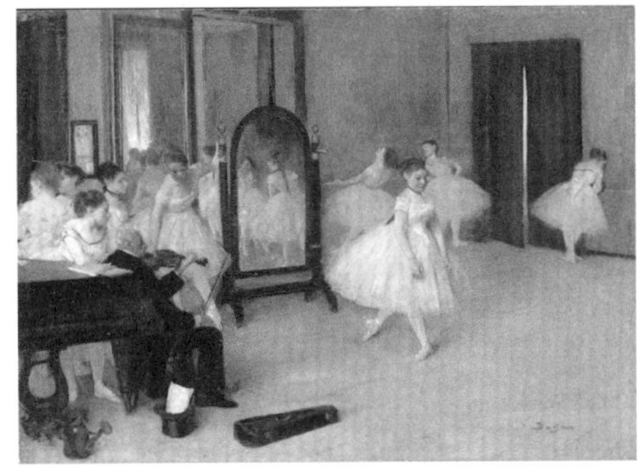

fig 4. Edgar Degas, The Dancing Class, ca. 1870, oil on wood, 19.7 × 27 cm, The Metropolitan Museum of Art, New York, H. O. Havemeyer Collection.

collector Louisine Havemeyer (1855–1929), artists such as Maurice Denis (1870–1943) and Suzanne Valadon (1865–1938), were aware of his sculptures, including the wax little dancer. Degas probably worked on it from 1878 to 1881. The model, Marie, was fourteen years old in 1878, and in view of the many preparatory studies that exist of the sculpture [fig. 5] it can be assumed that he had worked on it a lot longer before he showed it to the public in 1881. Marie posed for the artist clothed as well as naked. A smaller nude study he made of the sculpture has survived; there is a copy of it in the collection of Kunstmuseum Den Haag [fig. 6].

Impressionist sculpture

It is difficult to speak of impressionist sculpture, because it was only a small part of the exhibitions of works by the Impressionists. Moreover, not all of these sculptures were impressionist in nature, toying with a degree of incompleteness, capturing movement or a play of light and dark through the use of patina.[12] Degas looked upon his statues in a similar way as he did with the drawings and paintings that he produced. Whereas earlier sculptors such as Antonio Canova (1757–1822) or Jean-Baptiste Carpeaux (1827–1875) captured the dance in silent poses or in an idealized or allegorical way, for Degas the dancer was a way of investigating movement. As in his drawings and graphic work he often made use of many studies of a specific position.[13] There was also a clear interaction between the media used, because he made numerous drawings for the sculpture of the dancer, in addition to wax models [fig. 7]. After Degas more sculptors would depict dancers, showing realistic movements and attention to the dynamism of the dance. Auguste Rodin (1840–1917), for example, made countless studies of the dancers Isadora Duncan (1877–1927) and Loïe Fuller (1862–1928). He also studied dancers from the Cambodian Royal ballet and the Japanese dancer Hanako, Ōta Hisa (1858–1946). And for the sculptor Émile-Antoine Bourdelle (1861–1929), Duncan was even his most important muse and the source of countless drawings.[14]

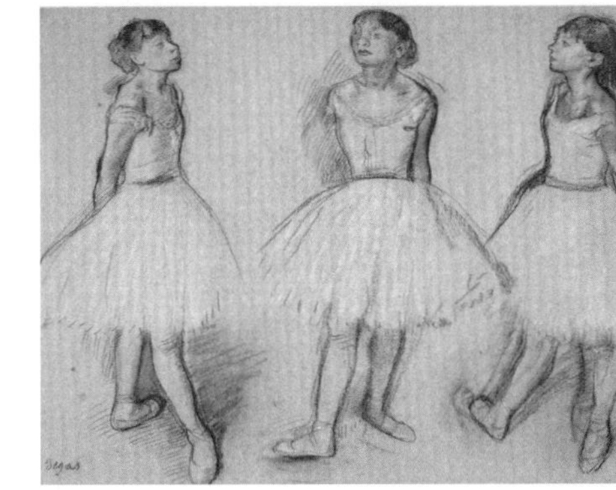

fig 5. Edgar Degas, Three Studies of a Dancer in Fourth Position, ca. 1879–80, charcoal and pastel with stumping, 48 × 61.6 cm, Art Institute Chicago.

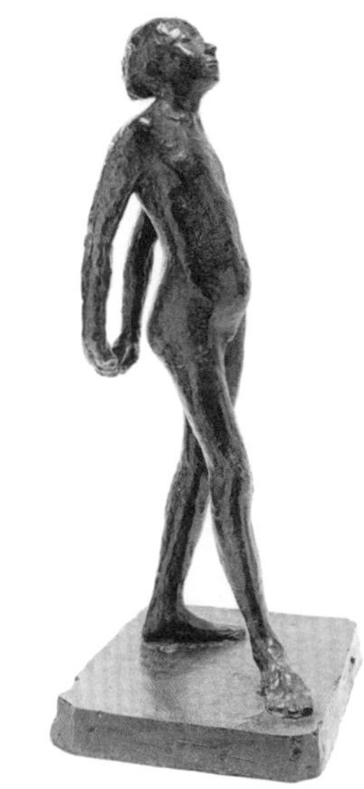

fig 6. Edgar Degas, Étude de nu pour la petite danseuse habillée, ca. 1878, cast bronze, 72 × 34 × 26 cm, Kunstmuseum Den Haag.

Artists and art dealers such as Paul Durand-Ruel (1831–1922) and Ambroise Vollard (1866–1939), who visited Degas's workshop, were impressed by the sculptures. Yet it remains unclear why he never exhibited them again.[15] They seem to have been an important part of his studio practice, where he regarded the wax statue as flexible, adjustable, and capable of remodelling if he did not like it, but not as definitive as bronze or marble. Vollard called to mind that he had once asked Degas if a statuette of a dancer could be cast in bronze, based on the autonomous quality he recognized in the statues, but on his return to the artist's workshop the day after, he saw that Degas had reduced it back to a formless ball of wax. For Degas, sculpture was a research process, rather than intended for sale.[16] Although the artist and the model maker Albino Palozzolo (1883–1973) did investigate the possibilities of casting the statues, it remained as just a few plaster casts during Degas's life.

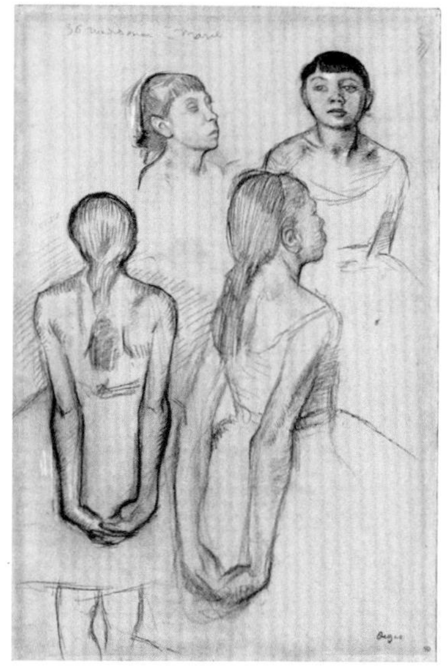

fig 7. Edgar Degas, Quatre études d'une danseuse, ca. 1878–1879, charcoal and white highlights on pink paper, 49 × 32 cm, RMN-Grand Palais (Musée d'Orsay), Paris.

Posthumous casts

In spite of the fact that he did not show them publicly, there actually was interest in the sculptures from potential clients. In 1903 Louisine Havemeyer wanted to buy the wax statue of the fourteen year-old dancer. The artist Mary Cassatt (1844–1926), a good friend of Degas, wrote about it to Durand-Ruel: "She will have nothing but the original, and she tells me that Degas, on the pretext that the wax has blackened, wants to do it all over in bronze or plaster with wax on the surface."[17] This seems to be at odds with Degas's opinion about his sculptures, because he did not want them executed in bronze, but it does add to the fact that he also covered the hair and the cloth body of the wax statue with wax. Be that as it may, the sale finally did not take place.[18]

After his death in 1917, Joseph Durand-Ruel (1862–1928) and Vollard got the commission to make an inventory of works which were still present in Degas's workshop. They were faced with an enormous amount of his own work and a sizeable art collection. In total there were more than 8,000 artworks, which were sold between 1918 and 1919 at five auctions of his own work and three of his collection. Degas had owned a great deal of work by friendly Impressionists and modern artists, like Vincent van Gogh (1853–1890), Édouard Manet (1832–1883) and Cézanne, and no fewer than 20 paintings and 80 drawings by Jean-Auguste Dominique Ingres (1780–1867), also great number of works of art by Eugène Delacroix (1798–1863). Eighty or so sculptures by Degas were found all over his living quarters at 6, Boulevard de Clichy, all executed in wax. Some of them were in a poor condition, many were provided with a steel armature that Degas had used for the modelling.[19] The wax sculptures were photographed by the photographer Gauthier between December 1917 and March 1918. There may have been adaptations made to some of the sculptures at that time, as some of the armatures had been removed.[20] The little dancer was also photographed [fig. 8].

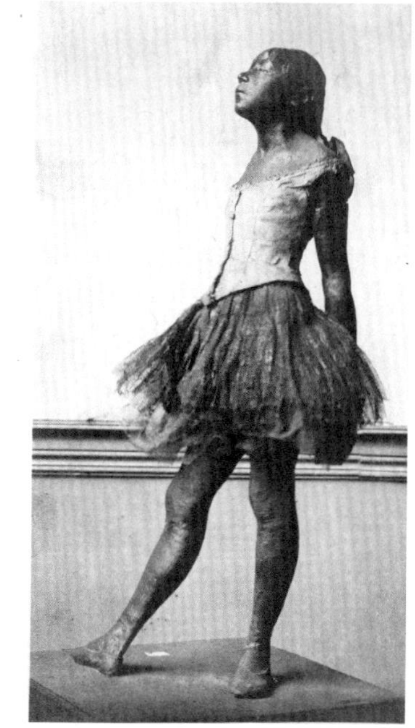

fig 8. Ambroise Vollard, Gauthier, Photo d'une sculpture en cire de Degas: Petite danseuse de 14 ans, ca. 1917, RMN-Grand Palais (Musée d'Orsay), Paris.

The decision to have copies of the wax statue made was finally taken by De Gas's heirs, because various people, including Cassatt, had warned them that it would be too hot in the workshop in the summer, and that the wax statues would melt.[21] She advised them to have them cast by an expert. The choice finally fell to the bronze caster Adrien A. Hébrard (1865–1937). The family negotiated a contract with him on 13 May 1918. The agreement was that 22 editions would be cast of it, 20 for sale, a set for the family [with the mark HER D] and a set for Hébrard [with the mark HER]. Hébrard also held on to a complete set, which was marked as 'Modèle'. The 20 copies to be sold were all given a letter from the alphabet. In certain cases Hébrard appears to have not kept to the agreed amount. Together with his daughter Nelly, he took care of the marketing and the sale of the sculptures. Some of the copies were cast again in the nineteen-fifties, but unfortunately there is no total summary.[22] We do know of 29 copies of the little dancer. In 1921 the heirs of De Gas wanted to gift a complete set to the Louvre, but it ultimately ended up in the Havemeyer Collection by way of Cassatt. At present two museums have a complete set. In 1929 the Metropolitan Museum in New York acquired series A, from a bequest by Havemeyer, and in 1930 the Louvre acquired series P (nowadays to be seen in Musée d'Orsay).

Different versions: the problem of the tutu

The original wax model which Degas showed in 1881 was formed over a metal armature, but it also contained iron wire, string, wood, clay, wax and other organic material.[23] It is clear that, among other things, the artist worked with material which was on hand in his workshop. The statue is now in the National Gallery of Art in Washington, as part of a gift from Paul Mellon (1907–1999) and his second wife Rachel Lambert Mellon (1910–2014) [fig. 9].[24] They acquired all 70 original wax sculptures, which had survived the casting process, in two parts, in 1956 and 1958. They donated 25 of them to the National Gallery of Art, the others ended up in the collections of the Virginia Museum of Fine Arts in Richmond, Musée d'Orsay in Paris and the Fitzwilliam Museum in Cambridge. For a long time it had been assumed that the wax models had been lost during the casting process of the bronze versions executed posthumously, because they were made using the lost wax method. In 1955, though, they were rediscovered and exhibited in the Knoedler Gallery in New York; they were subsequently bought by Mellon.[25] Evidently two wax models were produced, which were made using a plaster cast or a gelatine mould of the original wax sculptures.[26] We know of two plaster versions of the little dancer, made by Palazzolo for Hébrard. One of them found its way into the collection of National Gallery of Art in Washington by way of Mellon. This statue was executed with a tutu and real ballet slippers [fig. 10]. Incidentally, the grandchildren of Edgar's brother, René De Gas, donated his sculpting tools and painters' palettes to the d'Orsay.

Even though Gauthier documented the *Little Dancer* with good photos in 1917/1918, the most fragile parts – the silk hair ribbon and the cloth tutu – of the sculpture have been interpreted differently over the years. The variations of them differ per museum collection. During the period in which not only the Metropolitan Museum in New York, but also Musée d'Orsay in Paris and the Jocelyn Art Museum in Omaha, Nebraska replaced the tutus of their dancers, there was even talk of a real 'tutu war'.[27] The restorations vary greatly in material expression, volume and length.

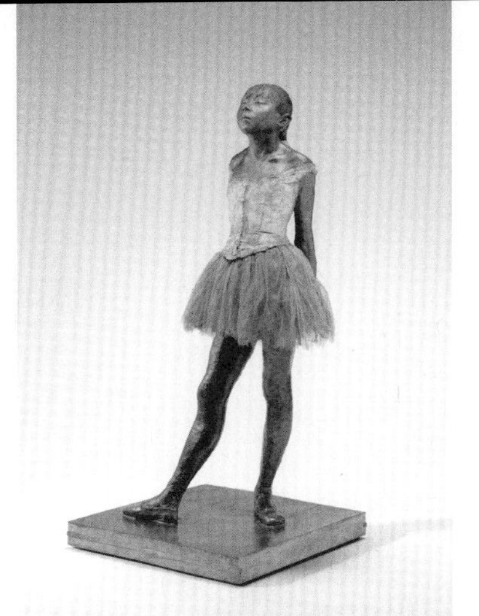

fig 9. Edgar Degas, *Little Dancer Aged Fourteen*, 1878–81, pigmented beeswax, 98.9 × 34.7 × 35.2 cm, National Gallery of Art Washington, collection of Mr. and Mrs. Paul Mellon.

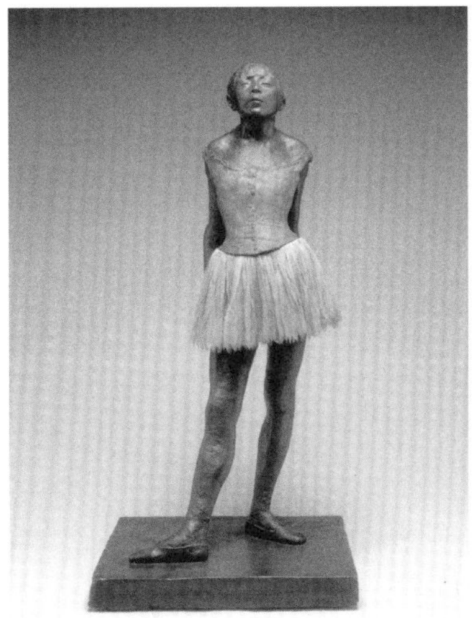

fig 10. Edgar Degas, *Little Dancer Aged Fourteen*, ca. 1920–21, painted plaster, 99.4 × 35 × 35.8 cm, National Gallery of Art Washington, collection of Mr. and Mrs. Paul Mellon.

The Metropolitan Museum in New York made a short documentary about the restoration process of 'their' tutu.[28] The most important question was whether it should be approached as a formal tutu as worn in dance performances, or as a garment worn during rehearsals. Presumably the latter, given that it is a young dancer in training. The Metropolitan's costume curator, Glenn Petersen, explains in the documentary that he felt some freedom to apply his own interpretation. The bronze cast was not the original statue exhibited in 1881.

The existing tutus were often quite dirty in colour, probably to match the now darkened colour of the wax. In addition, the fabric had become old and frayed. The version that Petersen made was already the fourth replacement. He studied tutus from Degas's time, from photographs and as he depicted them in his paintings. Petersen decided to make the skirt longer to better match the tutus that were worn during dance rehearsals in Degas's paintings. White fabric, as he described it in contemporary reviews, would contrast too strongly with the colour of the bronze, so he chose a dark beige colour and added some tinges of colour to it. He made the ribbon again, also darker in colour.

The tutu of the dancer in the Musée d'Orsay, by contrast, was reconstructed in 1998 in consultation with dressmakers from the Paris Opéra and is much shorter [fig. 11]. The first proposal was a straight tutu, but in the end a tutu of light pink tarlatan was chosen, draped in slightly staggered layers over each other.[29] The restoration of the one by the Albertinum in Dresden was also preceded by an in-depth research process.[30] Even the tutu around the original wax figure in the National Gallery of Art in Washington is no longer original. An online publication of research into the conservation of the wax figure discusses the issues surrounding the decision to replace or modify the tutu in detail.[31]

The tutu and ribbon of the sculpture from Museum Boijmans Van Beuningen have also been conserved and renewed several times. The tutu, whose fabric had become dirty and worn, was recreated in 1995 by the restorer Louis Damen and his wife Esther van Holk. They worked on the skirt for fourteen months

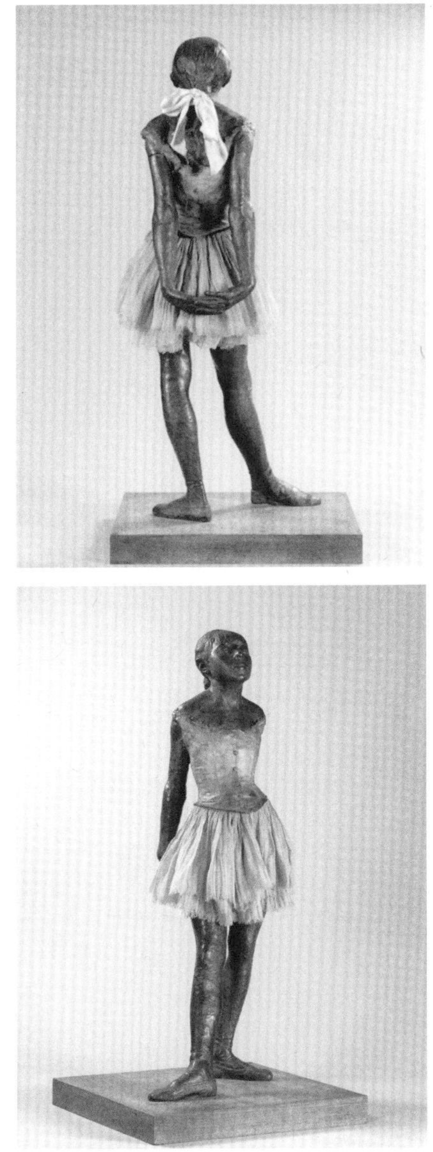

fig 11. Edgar Degas, *Petite danseuse de quatorze ans*, ca. 1921–1931, patinated bronze, 103.8 × 48.8 × 50 cm, Musée d'Orsay, Paris.

and decided to make it longer than the one that formed part of the acquisition in 1939 [fig. 12]. In an interview with Maasstad they explained that they too had conducted research into the length of the skirt in Degas's time. The original skirt was made after his death by a niece of Degas's, Jeanne Fevre.[32] The restorers concluded that this skirt had therefore also been an interpretation.[33] The National Ballet's costume department advised them to use tarlatan for the skirt, a type of sheer, cotton gauze, which consists of several layers. The choice of the soft green colour was based on the description of the dancer by Huysmans, who mentioned a grey-green (vert poireau) skirt in his review.[34] Under the tutu, knickers made of the same fabric and a few layers of tulle were added to make the skirt puff out a little.

The hair ribbon was replaced several times, in 1995 as well, because the old ribbon had fallen apart due to age. But in 2011 it was replaced again, with a darker satin one, which the restorer Saskia Rijsdijk washed and crumpled up to make it look older.[35] Nevertheless, the ribbon contrasts somewhat with the much darker tutu, which seems to have lost some of its volume and has become darker in colour over time. The museum may replace the skirt again in the future. Then the question will be asked again about how the skirt should be made and how faithful and authentic this execution should be. Will Museum Boijmans Van Beuningen follow one of the other renewed versions [figs. 13, 14] or will another decision be taken based on recent research?

The wooden base has been retained in most cases (it bears the mark of the Hébrard foundry), but the sculpture is not always shown in a display case. It would be interesting to find out why Degas had actually done it. Was it because of the fragility of the material or because he suspected that visitors would want to touch it? Presumably it had a more formal meaning. In any case, the display case was also ordered for the fifth Impressionism exhibition, where he initially planned to display the sculpture, but decided against it at the last moment.

Degas's sculptures have become even more famous since the rediscovery of the wax models in the nineteen-fifties. In 1956, the Virginia Museum of Fine Arts in Richmond was the first

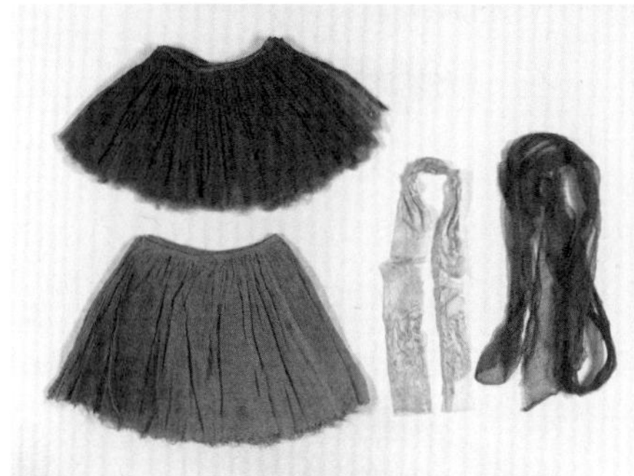

fig 12. Skirt and silk ribbon, 1939, collection Museum Boijmans Van Beuningen, Rotterdam.

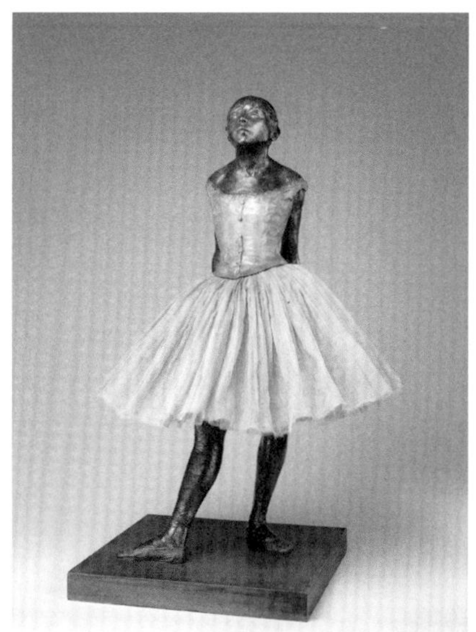

fig 13. Edgar Degas, The Little Fourteen-Year-Old Dancer, 1922, partially tinted bronze, 97.8 × 43.8 × 36.5 cm, The Metropolitan Museum of Art, New York, H. O. Havemeyer Collection.

to stage an exhibition that charted the relationship between the wax models and the later bronzes. Degas' dancer, once written about with disdain, became a world-famous sculpture. Whether it gives the same experience to the contemporary museum audience as it did to the nineteenth-century visitors to the Impressionist exhibition, is of course the question. What remains special is the vulnerability of the girl, who stands loosely in the fourth position: her age on the border between youth and adulthood, her imperfection, her apparent indifference, but also her strength.

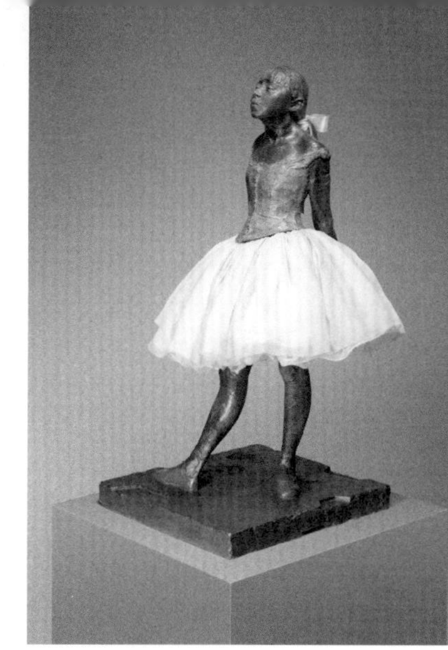

fig 14. Edgar Degas, Little Dancer Aged Fourteen, 1878–81 (1920–21), painted plaster, 99.1 × 49.5 × 50.8 cm, The Joslyn Art Museum Omaha Nebraska, gift of M. Knoedler & Co.

1 This was the Rondom Rodin, Tentoonstelling Honderd Jaar Fransche Sculptuur, staged by Hans Ludwig , C. Jaffé and others including John Rewald, 30 June 1939–2 January 1940.
2 '[...] men zal allereerst geneigd zijn plezier te hebben aan de arrogante houding van dit balletratje, dat eigenlijk nog maar een muis is.' Rotterdamsch Nieuwsblad, 12 January 1940, p. 2.
3 Anne Pingeot, 'Il faut recourir aux trois dimensions', in Pingeot and Horvat 1991, pp. 19-31.
4 Martine Kahane, Little Dancer, Aged Fourteen – The Model, in Czestochowski and Pingeot (ed.) 2002, pp. 101-107, pp. 103-104. In an article of February 1882 in L'Evenement, in which she is mentioned as an artist's model; it also stated that she regularly visited entertainment venues with a dubious reputations, such as Le Rat Mort.
5 New Haven and London 1998, p. 17.
6 Idem, pp. 4-5.
7 Anne Pingeot, 'Il faut recourir aux trois Dimensions', in Paris 1991, pp. 19-31 and p. 188.
8 'Ce n'était pas assez de la couleur. Il leur faut le cire, ou le plâtre ou le bronze. Nous allons voir, bone Deus! Des sculpteurs impressionistes', Jules Claretie, 'La Vie a Paris. Les Artistes Independantes', Les Temps (5 April 1881), cited in Frankfurt 2020, p. 48.
9 Alison Luchs, 'Degas's Little Dancer', National Gallery of Art, exhibition brochure 2014, p. 7.
10 'Expositions des artistes independants', La Chronique des arts at de la curiosité (16 April 1881): 1, cited in New Haven and London 1998, p. 21.
11 Luchs 2014, p. 7.
12 See Kisters, 'Licht, materie en perceptie: impressionistische beeldhouwkunst', in Amsterdam 2024, pp. 184-191.
13 Czestochowski, 'Degas's Sculpture Re-examined: The Marketing of a Private Pursuit', Czestochowski and Pingeot (ed.) 2002, pp. 11-25, p. 11.
14 In 2009 the Musée Bourdelle in Paris devoted an exhibition to the many drawings he made of her. https://www.bourdelle.paris.fr/en/visit/exhibitions/isadora-ducan-1877–1927
15 Frankfurt 2020, p. 52.
16 Roland Pickvance, 'Degas beeldhouwer', in Zwolle and Amsterdam 1988, pp. 17-22, pp. 18-19.
17 Letter 1903 from Cassatt and Durand-Ruel cited by Daphne Barbour, 'Degas's Little Dancer. Not Just a Study in the Nude', in Art Journal, summer 1995, pp. 28-32, p. 31. See also Pingeot and Horvat 1991, p. 189.
18 Opinions differ about the reasons. Possibly she thought that the condition of the wax statue was not at its best, but it could also be that Degas did not want to sell the original, but just a copy of it and that Havemeyer did not agree to that, see https://www.metmuseum.org/art/collection/search/196439 (consulted 7 May 2025).
19 Czestochowski, 'Degas's Sculpture Re-examined: The Marketing of a Private Pursuit', in Czestochowski and Pingeot (ed.) 2002, pp. 11-25, p. 12.
20 Ibid., p. 15.
21 The family name is usually written as De Gas or de Gas, whereas Edgar always signed his name as Degas.
22 This is explained in gretaer detail in the 2002 catalogue raisonné of the sculptures.
23 Arthur Beale, 'Little Dancer Aged Fourteen: The Search for the Lost Modèle, in New Haven and London 1998, pp. 97-108.
24 See https://www.nga.gov/research/publications/online-editions/conservation-publication/original-state (consulted 7 May 2025).
25 Czestochowski, 'Degas's Sculpture Re-examined: The Marketing of a Private Pursuit', in Paris 1991, pp. 11-25, p. 19.
26 Beale in New Haven and London, p. 103.
27 https://www.nga.gov/research/publications/online-editions/conservation-publication/original-state (consulted 9 May 2025), part of a bigger researchproject https://www.nga.gov/research/publications/modeling-movementdegas-dancers
28 See https://www.metmuseum.org/about-the-met/conservation-and-scientific-research/conservation-stories/2020/degas-dancer (consulted 5 May 2025).
29 Delpine Pinasa, 'Le tutu', Le revue du Musée d'Orsay 48/14 (autumn 1998) 7, pp. 63-65.
30 https://www.icon.org.uk/resource/the-world-s-most-famous-tutu.html (consulted 9 May 2025).
31 https://www.nga.gov/research/publications/modeling-movement-degas-dancers (consulted 15 May 2025), unknown author.
32 Lukas Gloor, 'Das Tutu der Kleinen 14jährigen Tänzerin von Edgar Degas – ein flüchtiges Gewebe', in Wuppertal 2016, pp. 300-43, p. 304.
33 Gervaise Frings, 'Veertien maanden werken aan een rokje', in Maasstad, 1 january 1995.
34 Esther van Holk in conversation with Nicole Bliek, 'Nieuwe tutu voor Degas' danseres', Algemeen Dagblad, 1 December 1994 and Esther van Holk, 'Een nieuwe tutu', in Wie wat bewaart... heeft een probleem. Bewaren en conserveren, 5 April 1995, pp. 35-38.
35 The fabric restorer Saskia Rijsdijk replaced the ribbon in 2011. See treatment report 16 August 2011 in MBVB object documentation. A short video was also made for ARTtube, https://www.youtube.com/watch?v=gWLWCci5OOE (consulted 15 May 2025).

Literature list

General:

Babour 1995 | Daphne Barbour, 'Degas's Little Dancer. Not Just a Study in the Nude', in Art Journal, summer (1995), pp. 28-32.

Czestochowski and Pingeot (ed.) 2002 | Joseph S. Czestochowski and Anne Pingeot (ed.), Degas Sculptures. Catalogue Raisonné of the Bronzes, Tokyo: The Torch Press and International Arts 2002.

Holk 1995 | Esther van Holk, 'Een nieuwe tutu', in Wie wat bewaart...heeft een probleem. Bewaren en conserveren, 5 April 1995, pp. 35-38.

Pinasa 1998 | Delpine Pinasa, 'Le tutu', Le revue du Musée d'Orsay 48/14 (autumn 1998) 7, pp. 63-65.

Exhibition catalogues:

Amsterdam 2024 | Fleur Roos Rosa de Carvalho and Sandra Kisters (ed.), 150 Years of Impressionism. The Light Breaks through in the Netherlands, exh. cat. Van Gogh Museum, Amsterdam, Bussum: Uitgeverij THOTH.

Amsterdam and Zwolle 1988 | Roland Pickvance, Degas Sculptor, exh. cat. Van Gogh Museum, Amsterdam and Zwolle: Waanders Uitgevers 1988.

Frankfurt 2020 | Alexander Eiling and Eva-Mongi-Vollmer (ed.), En passant. Impressionism in Sculpture, exh. cat. Städel Museum Frankfurt, Munich, London, New York: Prestel Verlag.

New Haven and Londen 1998 | Richard Kendall, Douglas W. Druick and Arthur Beale, Degas and the Little Dancer, tent, cat. Joslyn Art Museum, Omaha, New Haven and London: Yale University Press 1998.

Paris 1991 | Anne Pingeot and Frank Horvat, Degas Sculptures, exh. cat. Réunion des Musées nationaux, Paris: Impremérie nationale Editions, 1991.

Washington D.C. 1984 | Charles Moffet, Degas, The Dancers, exh. cat. National Gallery of Art Washington D.C. 1984.

Washington D.C. 2014 | Alison Luchs, 'Degas's Little Dancer', National Gallery of Art, Washington D.C. exhibition brochure 2014.

Wuppertal 2016 | Gerhard Finckh (ed.), Edgar Degas – Auguste Rodin. Wettlauf der Giganten zur Moderne, exh. cat. Von der Heydt Museum Wuppertal and Musée Rodin Paris 2016.

Online sources:

https://www.delpher.nl

https://www.metmuseum.org/art/collection/search/196439

https://www.metmuseum.org/about-the-met/conservation-and-scientific-research/conservation-stories/2020/degas-dancer

https://www.nga.gov/features/modeling-movement/little-dancer-history-of-the-project.html

https://www.icon.org.uk/resource/the-world-s-most-famous-tutu.html

Een nieuwe strik voor een danseresje: De restauratie van het danseresje van Edgar Degas (https://www.youtube.com/watch?v=gWLWCci5OOE).

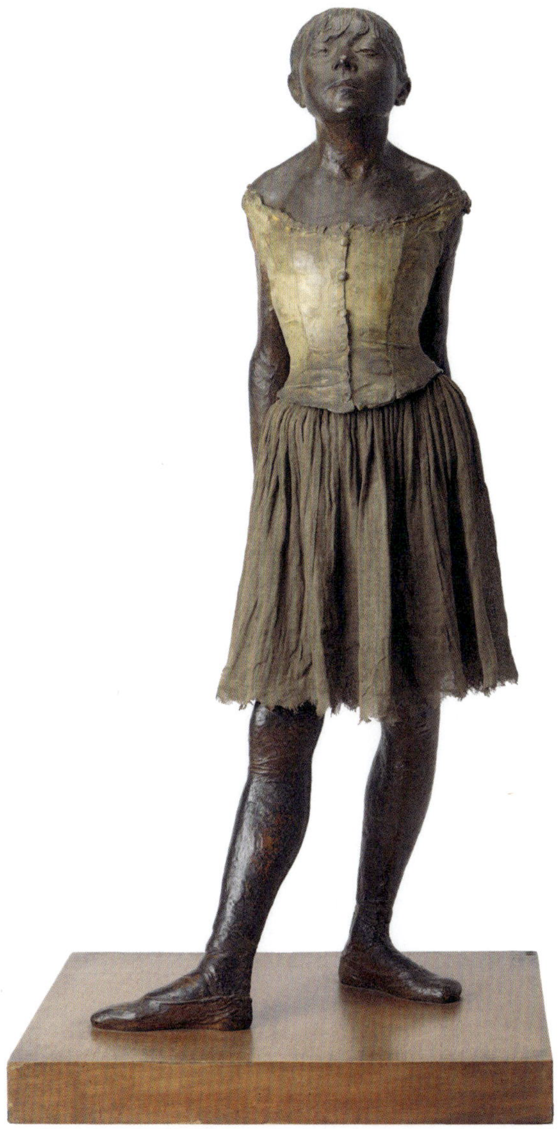

Edgar Degas (1834–1917), Petite danseuse de quatorze ans, 1880–1881 (1922)

Bronze and textile, 98 × 49 x 50 cm

Collection Museum Boijmans Van Beuningen, Rotterdam. Lend Stichting Museum Boijmans Van Beuningen. Inv.nr: BEK 1239 (MK)

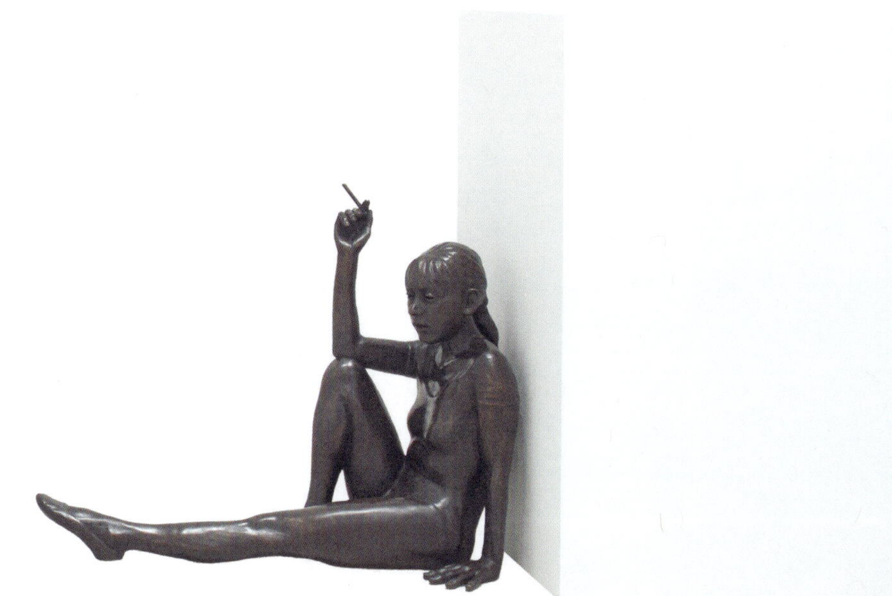

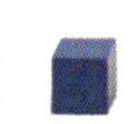

Ryan Gander (1976), I don't blame you, or, When we made love you used to cry and I love you like the stars above and I'll love you like the stars above and I'll love you 'til I die, 2008

Bronze, wood, ballerina: 50 × 60 × 125 cm, cube: 2 × 2 × 2 cm, plinth: 50 × 80 × 50 cm

Burger Collection, Hong Kong

"THE ARTIST SHOWS THAT A STATUE DOESN'T ALWAYS HAVE TO BE ON A PEDESTAL."
KAYLIN, 14 YEARS OLD

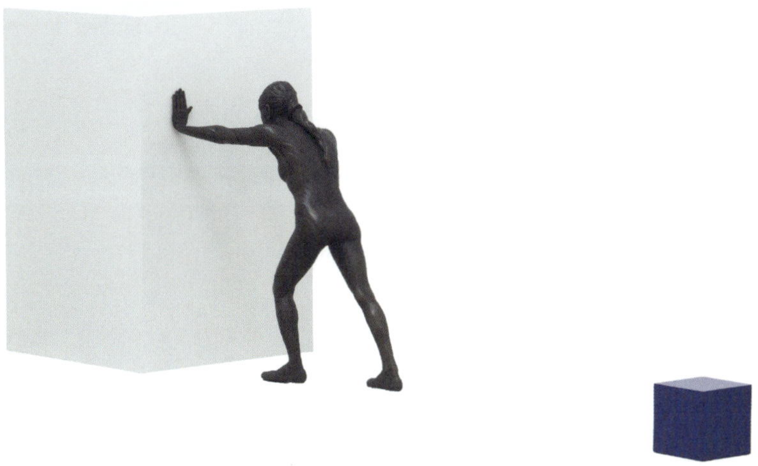

Ryan Gander (1976), Even though it's wrong, or, And I dreamed your dream for you and now your dream is real how can you look at me as I was just another one of your deals?, 2009

Bronze, wood, ballerina: 85 × 41 × 71 cm, cube: 17 × 17 × 17 cm, plinth: 100 × 50 × 60 cm

Private Collection, The Netherlands

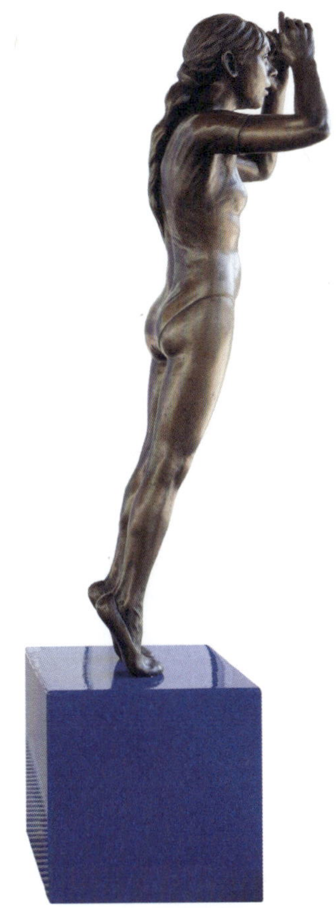

Ryan Gander (1976), Come up on different streets, they both were streets of shame, or, Absinth blurs my thoughts, I think we should be moving on, 2009

Bronze, wood, ballerina: 98 cm, cube: 30 × 30 × 30 cm, plinth: 40 × 100 × 40 cm

The Ekard Collection

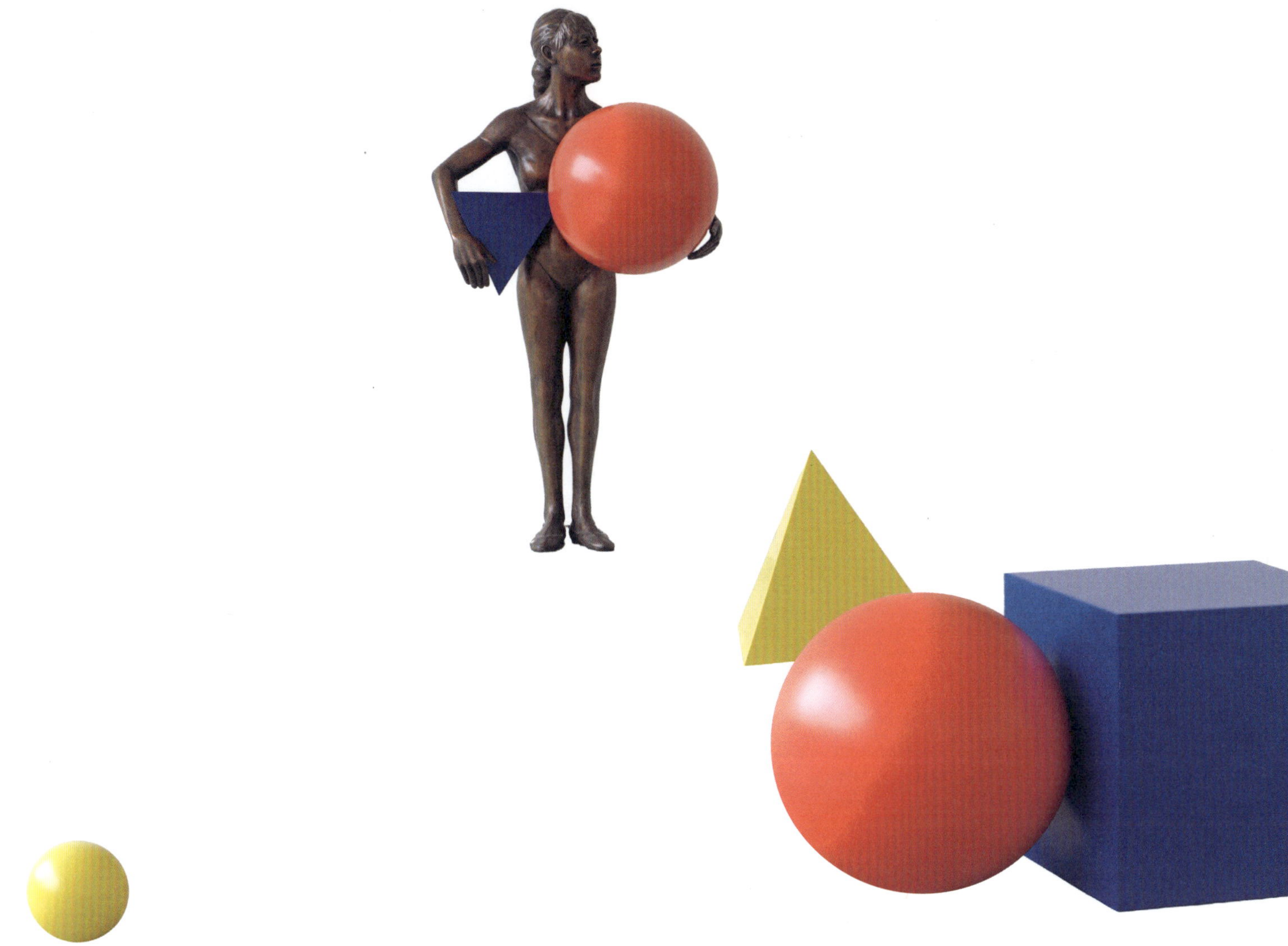

Ryan Gander (1976), You walk into a space, any space, or, Poor little girl beaten by the game, 2010

Bronze, steel, wood, ballerina: 30 × 100 × 30 cm, shapes: variable

Zabludowicz Collection

"THE ARTIST USES REALLY LONG POETIC TITLES TO GET VISITORS TO DELVE DEEPER AND THINK ABOUT THESE ARTWORKS."
QINGYAN, 14 YEARS OLD

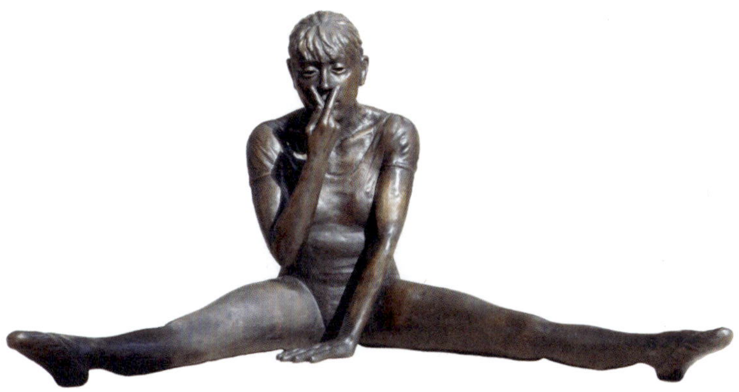

Ryan Gander (1976), Tight and formless thinking, or, Don't you know it's dark outside?, 2010

Bronze, wood, ballerina: 91 × 47 × 48 cm, cube: 10 × 10 × 10 cm, plinth: 25 × 40 × 25 cm

Obayashi Collection

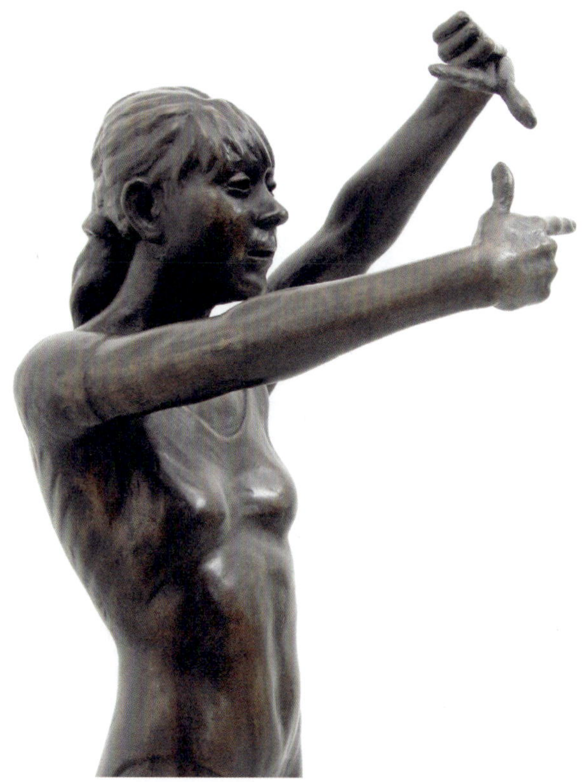

Ryan Gander (1976), The Observatory, or, It's not that it's bad, it's just that you're confused, 2011

Bronze, wood, ballerina: 25 × 100 × 37 cm, cube: 2.5 × 2.5 × 2.5 cm, plinth: 6 × 10 × 6 cm

Ishikawa Foundation, Okayama

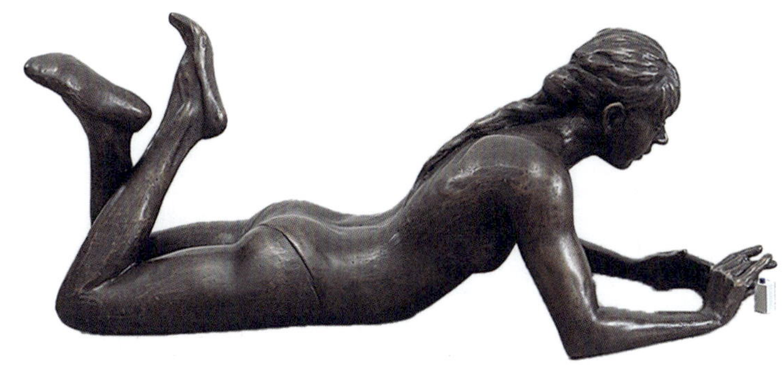

Ryan Gander (1976), You ruin everything (The economy of zero's), 2011

Bronze, wood, steel, ballerina: 31 × 33 × 80 cm, cube: 0.5 × 0.5 × 0.5 cm, plinth: 1.5 × 3 × 1.5 cm

Collezione De Iorio

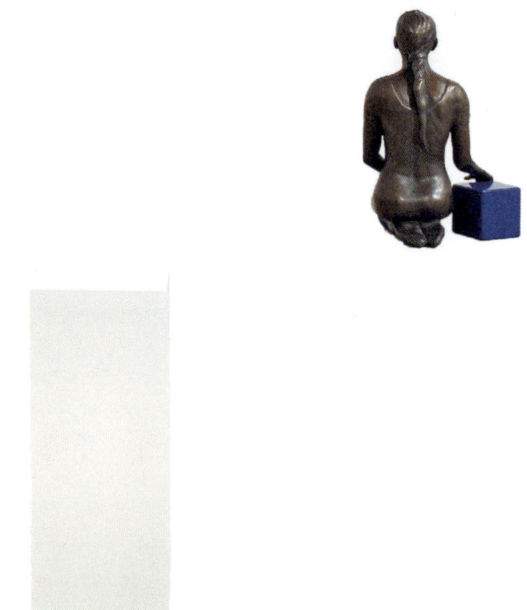

Ryan Gander (1976), Fortune on a string, or, Your eloquent works appear like a stuttering, 2011

Bronze, wood, ballerina: 55 × 38 × 29 cm, cube: 10 × 10 × 10 cm, plinth: 45 × 20 × 20 cm

Private Collection

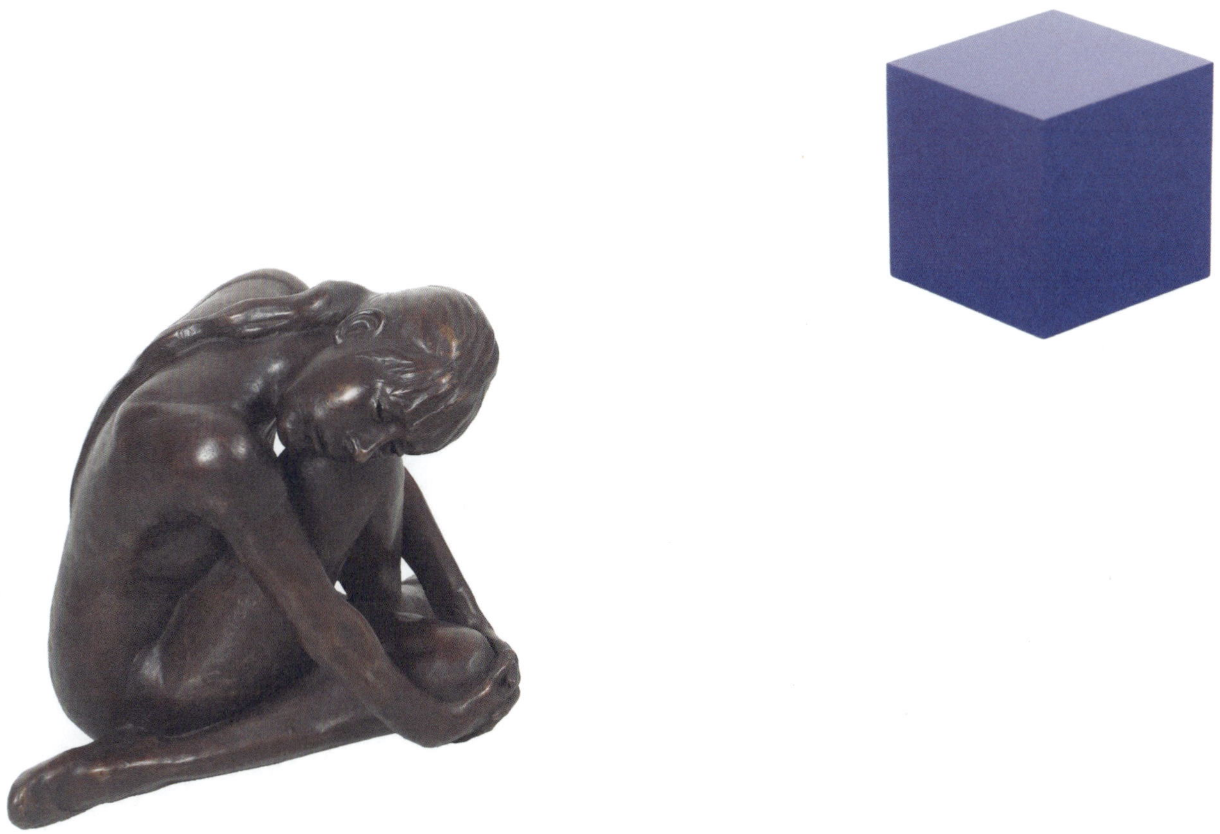

Ryan Gander (1976), Epiphany...learnt through hardship, 2012

Bronze, wood, ballerina: 100 × 25 × 12 cm, cube: 20 × 20 × 20 cm, plinth: 40 × 100 × 40 cm

Art Discovery Limited

Ryan Gander (1976), A picture is worth ten words, max, 2013

Bronze, wood, ballerina: 35 × 92 × 15 cm, cube: 8 × 8 × 8 cm, plinth: 35 × 65 × 35 cm

Private Collection

"I THINK THE ARTIST MADE THESE STATUES TO SHOW THAT DANCING CAN SOMETIMES MAKE YOU FEEL SAD WHEN THINGS DON'T WORK OUT AND THEN YOU START TO THINK ABOUT THINGS TOO MUCH, AND YOU CAN FEEL A BIT 'DOWN'."

MADELIEF, 14 YEARS OLD

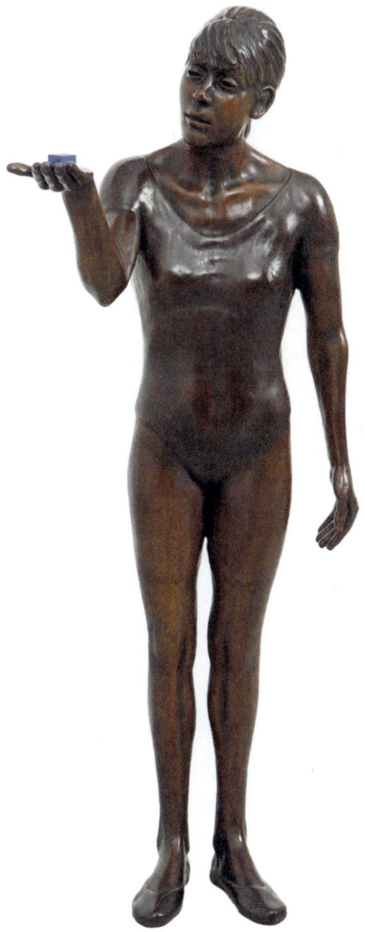

Ryan Gander (1976), Bleak Endings and Eve Online, or, Ryandóttir, 2013

Bronze, wood, ballerina: 96 × 36 × 33 cm, cube: 2 × 2 × 2 cm, plinth: 0.5 × 0.5 × 1.2 cm

Dazaifu Tenmangu

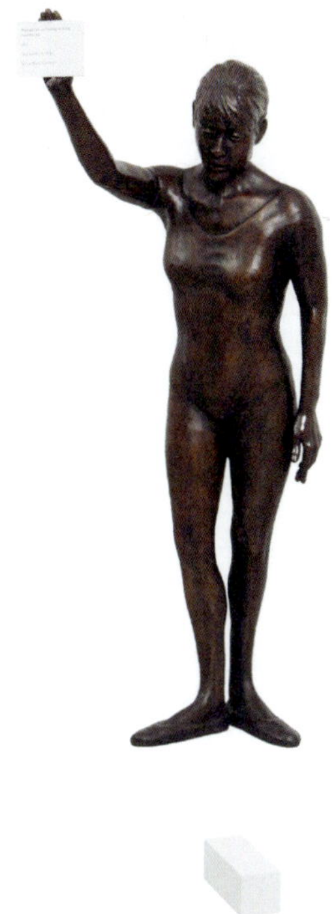

Ryan Gander (1976), Mordant wit, or, Trading on being misanthropic, 2013

Bronze, wood, ballerina: 105 × 27 × 40 cm, cube: 0.5 × 0.5 × 0.5 cm, plinth: 5 × 5 × 12 cm

Ishikawa Foundation, Okayama

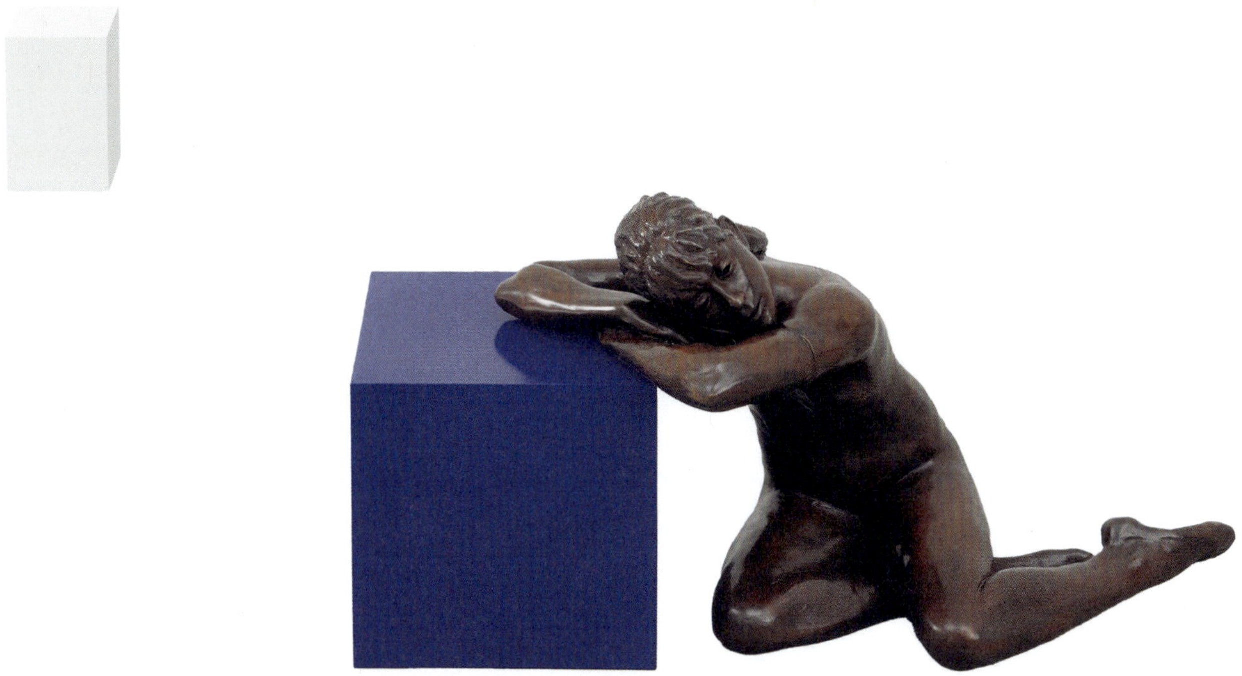

Ryan Gander (1976), To loving beyond our means, or, Armed with razor-sharp wit, 2015

Bronze, wood, ballerina: 43 × 88 × 38 cm, cube: 27 × 27 × 27 cm, plinth: 12,5 × 20 × 12,5 cm

Direct Art Collection (DAC)

"I THINK THE ARTIST CHOSE THOSE TITLES TO GET THE VIEWER TO THINK ABOUT THE TITLE IN CONNECTION WITH THE STATUE."
STORM, 14 YEARS OLD

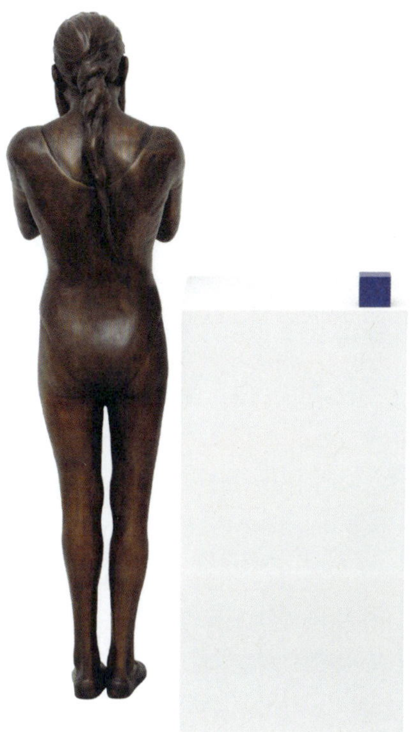

Ryan Gander (1976), Merchant of light, or, Holding hands with academia to the point where we're all kissing, 2015

Bronze, wood, ballerina: 23,5 × 93,5 × 20 cm, cube: 4 × 4 × 4 cm, plinth: 28,5 × 57 × 28,5 cm

Fondation Louis Vuitton, Paris

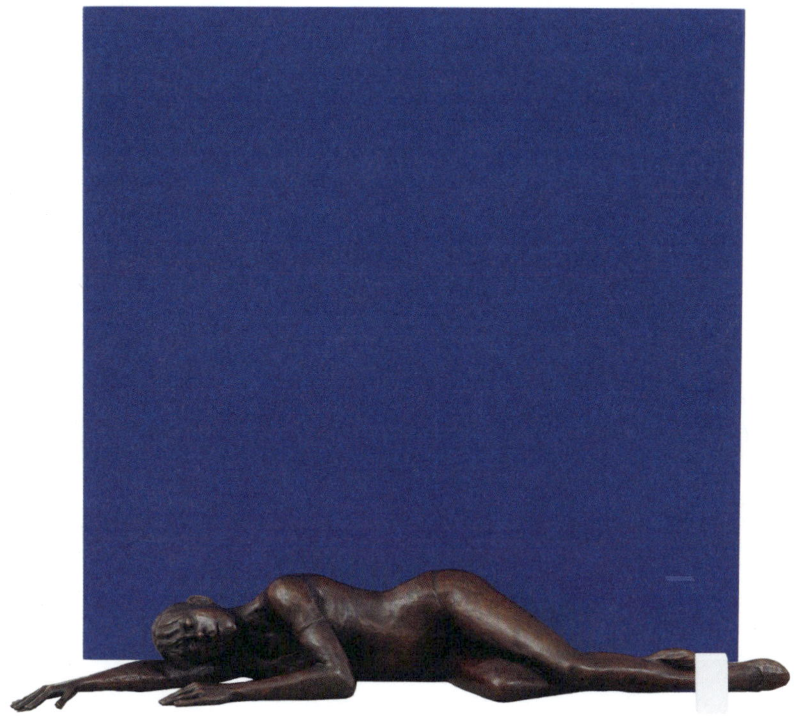

Ryan Gander (1976), As old as time itself, slept alone, 2016

Bronze, wood, ballerina: 116 × 19 × 30 cm, cube: 10 × 10 × 10 cm, plinth: 4 × 8 × 4 cm

Arts Council Collection, Southbank Centre, London

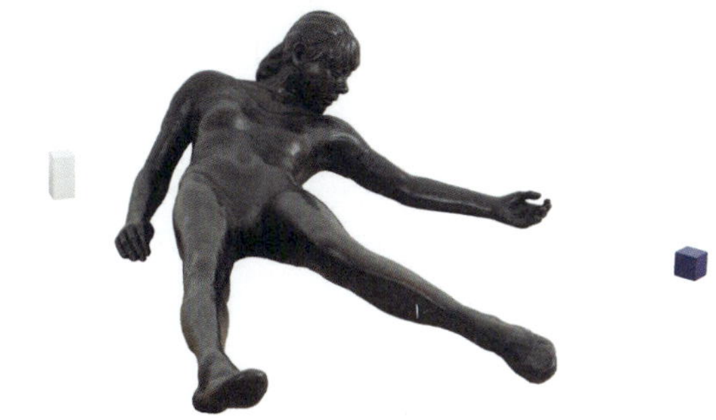

Ryan Gander (1976), To give life, or, Sympathetic String, 2017

Bronze, wood, ballerina: 78 × 28 × 86 cm, cube: 3.2 × 3.2 × 3,2 cm, plinth: 3.2 × 6.4 × 3.2 cm

Fondation Louis Vuitton, Paris

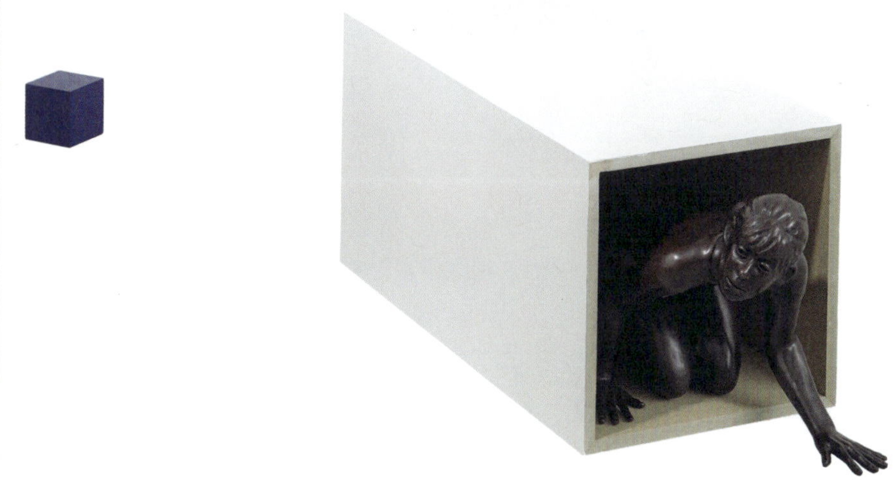

Ryan Gander (1976), Local and global reaching out, or, And sailed back over a year, And in and out of weeks, And through a day, 2017

Bronze, wood, ballerina: 38 × 38 × 62 cm, cube: 10 × 10 × 10 cm, plinth: 80 × 40 × 40 cm

Haidas Collection

"I RECOGNIZE MYSELF IN SOME OF THE BALLERINAS' POSITIONS, JUST LIKE WHEN I'M SOMETIMES SITTING OR LYING DOWN AT HOME."
NOURHANE, 14 YEARS OLD

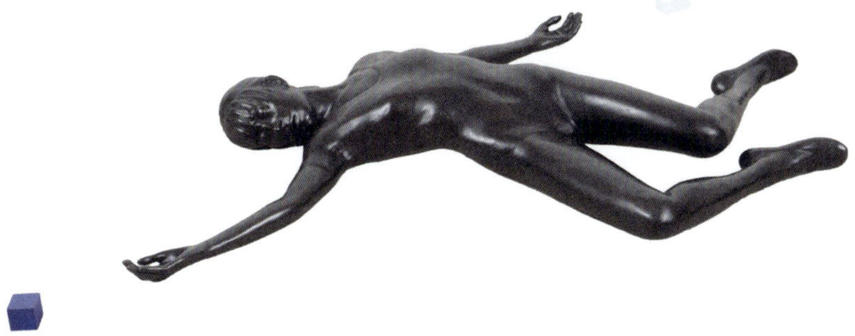

Ryan Gander (1976), Disenchantment on a visceral level, or, Play Signals, 2017

Bronze, wood, ballerina: 104 × 14 × 68 cm, cube: 3.2 × 3.2 × 3.2 cm, plinth: 2 × 5 × 2 cm

Courtesy the artist and Esther Schipper, Berlin/Paris/Seoul

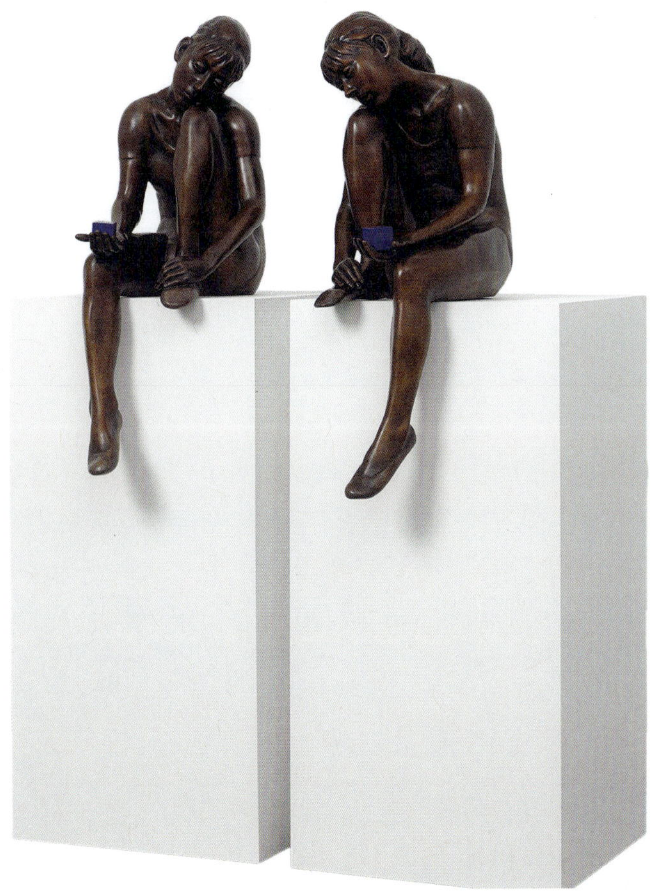

Ryan Gander (1976), All things being equal, or, I'm with you, 2018

Bronze, wood, ballerina: 70 × 25 × 35 cm, cube: 3 × 3 × 3 cm, plinth: 40 × 80 × 40 cm

Ryan Gander; Courtesy of Lisson Gallery

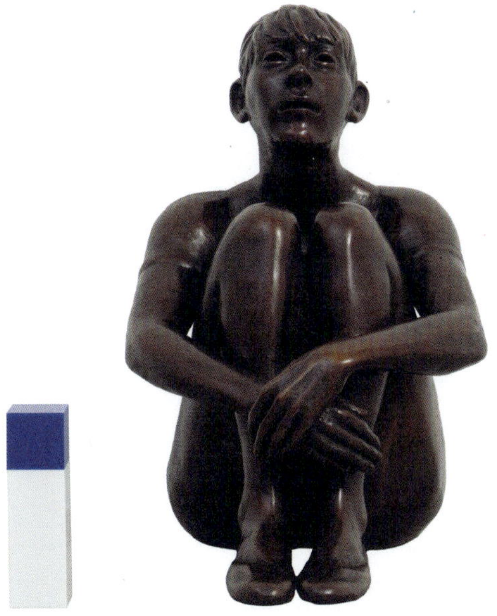

Ryan Gander (1976), Irretrievably broken from the past, or, Low hanging fruit, 2021

Bronze, wood, ballerina: 30 × 42 × 40 cm, cube: 4 × 4 × 4 cm, plinth: 4 × 10 × 4 cm

Ryan Gander; Courtesy of Lisson Gallery

Ryan Gander (1976), Waiting for timefall, or, Living in a time where everything is possible, but nothing can happen, 2025

Bronze, wood, ballerina: 47 × 43 × 33 cm, cube: 50 × 50 × 50 cm, plinth: 25 × 50 × 25 cm

Collection Museum Beelden aan Zee

"LIKE DEGAS'S, GANDER'S BALLERINAS ARE SOMETIMES LOST IN THOUGHT."
AMALIA, 14 YEARS OLD

Cover
Edgar Degas, Petite danseuse de quatorze ans, 1880–1881 (1922). Collection Museum Boijmans Van Beuningen, Rotterdam. Loan Stichting Museum Boijmans Van Beuningen. Photo: Studio Tromp. Ryan Gander, A picture is worth ten words, max, 2013. Private collection. Photo: Studio Gerrit Schreurs. © Ryan Gander c/o Pictoright Amsterdam 2025.

pp. 1-20
Studio Gerrit Schreurs. © Ryan Gander c/o Pictoright Amsterdam 2025.

30 Photo: Jay Russel
36 Loan by Stichting Museum Boijmans Van Beuningen, 1939. Photo: Studio Tromp.
37 fig 1: Loan by Stichting Museum Boijmans Van Beuningen, 1939. Photo: Studio Tromp.
fig 2: Collection Museum Boijmans Van Beuningen, Rotterdam. Photo: Tom Haartsen.
38 fig 3: Collection Museum Boijmans Van Beuningen, Rotterdam. Photo: Tom Haartsen.
39 fig 4: H. O. Havemeyer Collection, Bequest of Mrs. H. O. Havemeyer, 1929, The Metropolitan Museum of Art.
40 fig 5: Bequest of Adele R. Levy, Arts Institute Chicago.
fig 6: Kunstmuseum Den Haag.
41 fig 7: © RMN-Grand Palais (Musée d'Orsay)
42 fig 8: © RMN-Grand Palais (Musée d'Orsay / Franck Raux.
43 fig 9: National Gallery of Art Washington, Collection of Mr. and Mrs. Paul Mellon.
fig 10: National Gallery of Art Washington, Collection of Mr. and Mrs. Paul Mellon.
44 fig 11: © Musée d'Orsay, Dist. RMN-Grand Palais. Photo: Patrice Schmidt.
45 fig 12: Collection Museum Boijmans Van Beuningen, Rotterdam. Photo: Studio Tromp.
fig 14: The Metropolitan Museum of Art, H. O. Havemeyer Collection, Bequest of Mrs. H. O. Havemeyer, 1929.
46 fig 14: The Joslyn Art Museum Omaha Nebraska, gift of M. Knoedler & Co.

49 Bruikleen Stichting Museum Boijmans Van Beuningen. Inv.nr: BEK 1239 (MK). Photo: Studio Tromp.
50 Courtesy the artist and Hayward Gallery London. Photo: Stephen White. © Ryan Gander c/o Pictoright Amsterdam 2025.
51 Photo: Dave Morgan. © Ryan Gander c/o Pictoright Amsterdam 2025.
Photo: Studio Gerrit Schreurs. © Ryan Gander c/o Pictoright Amsterdam 2025.
52 Photo: Ken Adlard. © Ryan Gander c/o Pictoright Amsterdam 2025.
53 Photo: Studio Gerrit Schreurs. © Ryan Gander c/o Pictoright Amsterdam 2025.
Photo: John Henry Newton. © Ryan Gander c/o Pictoright Amsterdam 2025.
54 Photo: Ilya Rabanovich. © Ryan Gander c/o Pictoright Amsterdam 2025.
Photo: Ken Adlard. © Ryan Gander c/o Pictoright Amsterdam 2025.
55 Photo: John Henry Newton. © Ryan Gander c/o Pictoright Amsterdam 2025.
56 Photo: Ryan Gander Studio. © Ryan Gander c/o Pictoright Amsterdam 2025.
57 Photo: Ryan Gander Studio. © Ryan Gander c/o Pictoright Amsterdam 2025.
Photo: Ryan Gander Studio. © Ryan Gander c/o Pictoright Amsterdam 2025.
58 Photo: Jack Hems. © Ryan Gander c/o Pictoright Amsterdam 2025.
59 Photo: Aurelien Mole. © Ryan Gander c/o Pictoright Amsterdam 2025.
Photo: Anna Arca. © Ryan Gander c/o Pictoright Amsterdam 2025.
60 Photo: Jack Hems. © Ryan Gander c/o Pictoright Amsterdam 2025.
Photo: Aurelien Mole. © Ryan Gander c/o Pictoright Amsterdam 2025.
61 Photo: Ryan Gander Studio. © Ryan Gander c/o Pictoright Amsterdam 2025.
Photo: George Darrell. © Ryan Gander c/o Pictoright Amsterdam 2025.
62 Photo: George Darrell. © Ryan Gander c/o Pictoright Amsterdam 2025.
Photo: Studio Gerrit Schreurs. © Ryan Gander c/o Pictoright Amsterdam 2025.

Exhibition
Ryan Gander X Edgar Degas – Pas de Deux
Artist
Ryan Gander
Director and Curator
Brigitte Bloksma
Exhibition design
Magali Snelder
Loaners
Stichting Museum Boijmans Van Beuningen, The Ekard Collection, Esther Schipper Gallery, Direct Art Collection (DAC), Ishikawa Foundation, Haidas Collection, Art Discovery Limited, Arts Council Collection, Fondation Louis Vuitton, Lisson Gallery, Obayashi Collection, Zabludowicz Collection, Burger Collection, Collezione De Iorio, various private collections.
Team Museum Beelden aan Zee
Joost Bergman, Dick van Broekhuizen, Lot Fakkeldij, Denise Hermanns, Renz Klerks, Stan Koppe, Stella Kramer, Maud Kurvers, Maud van der Meer, Julija Novovic, Loes Ris, Karlien Ritter, Jacquelien van Schaik, Robbert Vonk, Godert de Vos van Steenwijk, Iris van der Zee and Heleen Zuthem van Lindenberg.
Decor and art handling
Jan Bokma, Thijs Ebbe Fokkens, Lucas van Eeden, Juan Giraldo, Robert Knoop, Lisa Sebestikova.
Thanks to
Ryan Gander Studio, Phil Mayer, Emily Bryson, Katherine Gardner, Freeman Abayasekera, Paul Baldwin, Wendy Ellis, Nick Elphick, Ann-Marie James, Ella Lockwood, Simon Newby, John Newton, Felix Wentworth, Annet Gelink Gallery, Sandra Kisters, Lydia Figes, LIDA Fonds, Business Members, Sculpture Club, Golden Members, Members, volunteers Museum Beelden aan Zee.

Catalogue
This publication is published on the occasion of the exhibition: Ryan Gander X Edgar Degas – Pas de Deux in Museum Beelden aan Zee from 20 June 2025 – 4 January 2026.

Publishers
Waanders Publishers, Zwolle, Museum Beelden aan Zee, The Hague
Authors
Brigitte Bloksma, Lydia Figes, Sandra Kisters
Project Lead - Catalogue
Karlien Ritter
Editorial & Visual Editor
Denise Hermanns, Stan Koppe and Dick van Broekhuizen
Translation
Phil Clarke (NL-ENG)
Thea Wieteler (ENG-NL)
Design
Linda van Deursen
Photography exhibition
Studio Gerrit Schreurs, Gerrit Schreurs and Naomi Kok
Lithography
Benno Slijkhuis, Wilco Art Books
Printing
Wilco Art Books, Amersfoort

ISBN 9789462626386
NUR 644
waanders.nl
beeldenaanzee.nl

Thanks to
Jan Linkens, Marishka van Loon and the contributions of the students from the Royal Conservatoire Dance in The Hague, Tim van Broekhuizen en the contributions of the students from the Maris College The Hague, and Ties Seyffert.

The exhibition in Museum Beelden aan Zee and this publication is made possible by

Partners

VRIENDENLOTERIJ

Don Quixote Foundation.

Sponsors

MOLSBERGEN DEVELOPMENT
LIDA FONDS
ZABAWAS
Den Haag
Zadelhoff Cultuurfonds
BLOCK BUSTER FONDS
VRIENDENLOTERIJ
het Cultuurfonds
VSBfonds.
VandenEnde FOUNDATION
mondriaan fonds
Stichting retourschip

Private Sponsors